Contents

Introduction **5**

Glossary and Abbreviations **6**

Phase I
    Auschwitz I (Main Camp) **7**

Phase II
    Birkenau (Death & Labour Camp) **63**

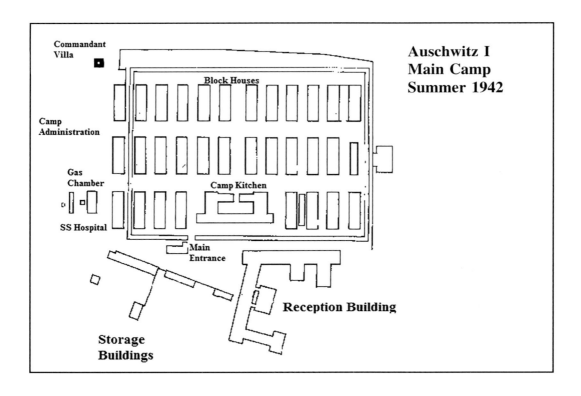

About the Author

Ian Baxter is a military historian who specialises in German twentieth century military history. He has written more than twenty books including *Afrika-Korps*; *Auschwitz Death Camp*; *Belsen and its Liberation*; *Blitzkrieg in the West*; *The Crushing of Poland*; *Final Days of the Reich*; *German Army on the Eastern Front – The Advance*; *German Army on the Eastern Front – The Retreat 1943–1945*; *German Guns of the Third Reich*; *Himmler's Nazi Concentration Camp Guards*; *Hitler's Defeat on the Eastern Front*; *Hitler's Headquarters 1939–1945*; *Hitler's Heavy Panzers 1943–45*; *Hitler's Mountain Troops 1939–1945: The Gebirgsjager*; *Hitler's Panzers*; *Nazi Concentration Camp Commandants 1933–1945*; *Panzer Divisions at War 1939–1945*; *Retreat to Berlin*; *The U-Boat War 1939–1945*; *Waffen-SS on the Eastern Front 1941–1945* and *Waffen-SS on the Western Front 1940–1945*. He has written over 100 journals including *Last days of Hitler, Wolf's Lair, Story of the V1 and V2 Rocket Programme, Secret Aircraft of World War Two, Rommel at Tobruk, Hitler's War with his Generals, Secret British Plans to Assassinate Hitler, SS at Arnhem, Hitlerjugend, Battle of Caen 1944, Gebirgsjäger at War, Panzer Crews, Hitlerjugend Guerrillas, Last Battles in the East, The Battle of Berlin*, and many more. He has also reviewed numerous military studies for publication, supplied thousands of photographs and important documents to various publishers and film production companies worldwide, and lectures to various schools, colleges and universities throughout the United Kingdom and Ireland.

Introduction

Using many contemporary rare and unpublished images this book is a photographic insight into Auschwitz-Birkenau today. With over 250 images the book shows in great detail the sheer size and scope of Auschwitz and the nearby Birkenau complex. It reveals how the buildings were constructed and then tells of the private firms that were employed by the SS to build them.

Accompanied with captions and text the book draws on key documents from the German Building Office showing the evolution of Auschwitz concentration camp using plans, letters, telegrams, work site labour reports, and minutes of meetings. It unveils how the SS needed civilian expertise to install heating, electrical, and sewage systems, to build chimneys, and to provide building shells. Many of these buildings are still standing today. It shows just how many civilian companies were involved, professionally cooperation in genocide, and reveals just how eager they were to produce the goods for the SS for financial reward.

The book shows the step-by-step transformation of the buildings including the crematoria and how these buildings aided the largest killing factory of all time. The reader will see for himself the extensive array of buildings comprising of the commandant's villa, prisoner reception building, prisoner barracks and huts, the delousing area known as the Sauna, the camp hospital, workshops, the kitchens, the SS administrative buildings, SS barracks, and the areas where the crematoria once stood, now lying in heaps of ruins – blown up by the SS in a last minute attempt to conceal their murderous activities before the arrival of the Red Army – now a shrine to the many hundreds of thousands that perished there.

The reader will quickly learn how pivotal the Auschwitz-Birkenau complex was, and how it became the Nazi centrepiece for forced labour and genocide. This book is a real addition to holocaust studies and is proof of the horrors that were inflicted on those that passed through the gates of Auschwitz-Birkenau.

* * *

The views or opinions expressed in this book, and the context in which the images are used, do not necessarily reflect the views or policy of, nor imply approval or endorsement by, the United States Holocaust Memorial Museum (USHMM).

Glossary and Abbreviations

General Government – Occupied part of eastern Poland not annexed to Germany.

Gestapo – Geheime Staatspolizei: state secret police.

Reichsführer-SS – Reich Chief of the SS and German Police.

RSHA Reichssicherheitshauptamt: Reich Main Security Office, formed in late 1939, uniting Gestapo, criminal police, SIPO and SD.

SD – Sicherheitsdienst: security service of the Nazi Party.

Sonderkommando – Special unit of SS.

SS – Schutzstaffel: Guard detachment created in 1925 as elite Nazi Party bodyguard that evolved into a security and intelligence service with a military arm.

Waffen-SS – Weapon SS: Military arm of the SS from 1939 onwards.

Wehrmacht – German armed forces.

WVHA – Wirtschafts und Verwaltungshauptamt: SS economic and administrative head office responsible for SS economic enterprises and concentration camps from 1942 under the command of Oswald Pohl.

Phase I

Auschwitz I

(Main Camp)

The German authorities quickly pressed forward to establish various camps in Poland where Polish prisoners could be incarcerated and set to work as stone-breakers and construction workers for buildings and streets. It was envisaged that these Poles would remain as a slave labour force, and it was therefore deemed necessary to erect these so called 'quarantine camps' in order to subdue the local population. Initially, it had been proposed that the quarantine camps were to hold the prisoners until they were sent to the various other concentration camps in the Reich. However, it soon became apparent that this purpose was impracticable so it was approved that these camps were to function as a permanent prison for all those that were unfortunate enough to have been sent there.

On 21 February 1940 a former labour exchange and artillery barracks near a small district town in Poland called Oświęcim had been deemed suitable for the so-called quarantine camps. The site was to be run by SS-Hauptsturmführer Rudolf Höss, and he was told that the camp should serve as a regional dumping ground for all Polish political prisoners so all these 'undesirables' could be transferred at a moment's notice to camps in the west as slave labourers.

The town of Oświęcim itself was situated in a remote corner of south-western Poland, in a marshy valley where the Sola River flows into the Vistula about 35 miles west of the ancient city of Kraków.

The location for the camp was a former Polish barracks. The accommodation consisted of eight two-storey and fourteen single-storey brick barracks framing the north and south sides of a large exercise yard which were able to be transformed into a prison camp with extra buildings. The location for the site was also deemed well situated for Auschwitz as it had very good railway connections and was isolated from outside observation. Although the water supply was polluted and there were mosquitoes everywhere, the Germans would be able to transform these swamped and infested marshes along the Vistula and Sola Rivers into what they envisaged as a valuable outpost of the Reich.

On 27 April, plans were approved for the construction and adaptation of the new site at Auschwitz. It was also agreed that it would house around 10,000 prisoners. On 4 May, Rudolf Höss was officially named as commandant of the new camp.

In order to construct and transform the new camp and adapt the twenty brick barracks for the inmates, Höss had been given a construction budget of 2 million Reich Marks. With this generous allowance he would be given the task of cleaning the existing barracks for the guards, rebuilding the two barracks outside the fence into officers' quarters and a hospital for the garrison, building a barrack for the Blockführer at the gate, constructing eight guard towers around the perimeter of the camp, building a hayloft, installing a crematorium in the abandoned powder magazine building, and tidying the three-storey house on the edge of the existing camp in order to make it habitable for him and his family. Initially Höss took up residence in a hotel overlooking the Auschwitz station while his family home was prepared. Here he would ponder on the future plans for the construction of the camp and spend 'all his waking hours' overseeing the developments.

During May and early June, construction of the camp progressed relatively slowly, but a fence with second-hand barbed wire was soon being installed around the perimeter, and new buildings began to be constructed. At the entrance of Auschwitz, Höss had a new steel gate forged in a hurriedly-built workshop and a frame built. Emblazoned along the top of the gate frame he had the inscription erected that he liked so much at Dachau: 'Arbeit Macht Frei' – 'Work Makes You Free'.

Throughout the early phase of building, more SS men were recruited as guards, and by 20 May, fifteen SS men arrived from the cavalry unit stationed in Kraków and were soon installed as part of the camp's guard garrison. During June an additional hundred SS were sent to reinforce the guard garrison along with SS officers and NCOs of various ranks.

The Auschwitz transit camp was gradually taking shape, but was far from completed. With the construction work barely begun, on 14 June a passenger train steamed into Auschwitz station from Tarnow prison carrying on board 728 political prisoners.

Throughout July and early August work continued on the camp, including the modification of the former powder magazine store, which started about 5 July. Its primary use was to be a crematorium, but was initially seen as being for delousing purposes. Before the crematorium was in operation those that died were transported to Gliwice and incinerated in the municipal crematorium. The conversion of the crematorium was undertaken by the full authorisation of the SS construction management. In fact, even before Höss had taken up his new post at Auschwitz the installation of a crematorium had already been decided. J.A. Topf and Sons of Erfurt, a company with a section specialising in the manufacture and installation of crematorium furnaces, headed by the chief engineer Kurt Prüfer, had been commissioned to undertake the first drawings. The plans showed the first furnace to be installed and gave full details of the internal structure. Schlachter, the camp's architect, had himself already obtained extensive information on the technology on the double muffler system, and the coke-heated furnace. He discussed this new equipment with Höss and the camp officials, and plans for its installation were agreed with SS headquarters in Berlin. Höss was in total agreement with the building of the crematorium at his new camp. After all, he looked upon the incineration of those who died at the camp as the simplest method to make the environment more hygienic.

The conversion of the building into a crematorium in July was undertaken relatively quickly, considering the lack of building materials at the camp. The installation consisted of one entrance on the northwest side and included a furnace room with two incinerators and a charnel house. The concrete roof was flat and the building was surrounded on three sides by earth embankments with openings for the window of the coke plant. There were two windows in the furnace room, which were installed to cool down the inside temperature of the building. An external chimney had been built and was connected to the furnaces by underground flues. The entrance to the crematorium was camouflaged by a very large concrete wall that enclosed the courtyard with two enormous wooden gates. In order to conceal the crematorium from view a one-storey building housing the SS hospital was constructed nearby along with the camp workshops and the barracks of the political department.

Besides the transformation of the former powder magazine store into a crematorium, work continued on various other buildings both inside and outside the camp. In order to speed the completion of the camp they desperately required building supplies. An order was sent from Berlin ordering that all Polish civilians living in the vicinity of the area of the site were to be removed from their homes and deported to forced labour camps. This having been done, teams were ordered into Auschwitz town to demolish all the empty houses for wood, bricks and anything else they might find useful.

In September Oswald Pohl from the SS Main Administration and Economic Office visited Auschwitz. Pohl had envisaged that Auschwitz would play a fundamental part in the concentration camp system in Upper Silesia and had already determined the economic future for the camp. He saw that the nearby sand and gravel pits could be easily incorporated into the SS-owned German Earth and Stone Works. It was therefore imperative for Pohl that the camp was running efficiently and the construction programme maintained with highest priority and within budget. Two weeks later, on 4 October, the first trainloads of materials arrived at the camp.

The labour force that continued building the camp lived and worked in appalling conditions. By October there was a mixture of inmates that consisted of Jews, members of the intelligentsia, resistance and political prisoners, together with Polish Catholic priests. All of them were struggling for survival and nothing was done to alleviate the dire conditions. Under-equipped, lacking protective gear, and mal-nourished, the inmates went about their place of work constantly being mentally and physically abused by the guards.

Within weeks the camp had been transformed. The commandant's office, a rather large imposing brick building which was generally used to deal with matters that affected the SS staff, had been constructed. It was primarily responsible for keeping all records and for supplying the garrison with weapons and other important military equipment. All transport and communications were controlled from this office. The office was divided into a number of different sections which included: office supply, communications office, judicial affairs, weapons, military supplies, and the engineer's office. Höss also had his own personal office and a boardroom where he and his staff gathered for meetings every Tuesday and Thursday morning. The head of the com-mandant's office was Höss's adjutant. His deputy was always a non-commissioned officer who also served as the 'Staff Sergeant of the Commandant's Office'.

The most important office next to the commandant's office was the adjutant's office. This office stood next door to the main commandant's office building and is where Höss's adjutant of Auschwitz, SS-Untersturmführer Josef Kramer worked and issued orders. Kramer made sure that all Höss's orders were carried out. He was responsible for all orders, promotions, various staff matters, issuing passes and would sign the letters. He often worked very closely with Höss and served as his deputy on regular occasions. Even at the weekly meetings on Tuesdays and Thursdays he was often seen seated next to Höss, and even personally chaired the meetings.

Another department that opened at the camp in 1940, and liaised with both the commandant's and adjutant's offices, was the Political Department or Gestapo offices. This small building was constructed next to the newly built crematorium, and was primarily used to deal with prisoner population and any issues relating to the camp itself and the SS staff. Its office maintained all prisoner records, registration of new arrivals, investigations, torturing, and supervising the executions of prisoners. It was also responsible for investigating corruption and fraud, the loss of official property and arresting and prosecuting SS men involved in neglect of duty or aiding an escape. In fact the Political Department was so powerful that it even had the authority to deal with SS headquarters in Berlin direct without it ever consulting Höss.

One particular building that Höss had been keen to get ready was the house in which he was to live with his family. By the summer of 1940 the house was deemed ready, in spite of the fact the exterior of the building was still in need of painting. The house, or the commandant's residence, but commonly known at the Auschwitz camp as the Höss villa, was an imposing two-storey building situated at the corner of the camp. The front of the building, with its large windows and small terrace, over-looked the Rajsko–Auschwitz road. There was a little untended garden to the front with a small brick wall and gate to the main entrance of the house. To the side of the building there was a double gate with a drive where vehicles could access the property. On the opposite side of the house, reached by a concrete path, was the tradesmen's entrance which consisted of a flight of concrete steps leading to the side door with a porch, overlooking the garden. The garden itself was predominantly situated to the side of the house and consisted of a number of trees and shrubberies from the previous occupants. A fence with barbed wire was erected around the perimeter of the garden and the house, in order to divide it from the main camp. In November new high concrete fencing was constructed and topped with barbed wire to replace the old fencing around the entire boundary of the camp. New fencing was also installed at the rear and sides of the Höss villa, making the house completely separate from the camp and virtually invisible from the garden, except for the roofs and chimneys of the commandant's office and administration buildings. The fence to the rear of the house, which hid the commandant's office, administration offices, SS guardhouse and the newly constructed crematorium, was further hidden by a large mound of earth placed behind the fence, and trees planted. Höss had been particularly insistent on trying to conceal the villa from the camp as much as possible, and made it known that he wanted his family to live in absolute privacy.

Inside the villa there were two floors. The first two flights of stairs were concrete, while the third was wooden leading up to a large attic. The house had plenty of space, with lots of adjoining rooms, but it was cold as there were no radiators installed. As soon as Höss's family arrived at the house that summer in 1940, Hedwig immediately set to work trying to make it as comfortable as possible for her husband and four children. She was thrilled at the prospect of living in such a large home and excited about choosing the various furnishings.

During the first week of October the first snow showers arrived in the camp, and this did nothing to alleviate Höss's unhappy disposition. There had been little preparation for the winter, but construction had to continue in spite of the thermometer plummeting to below zero. The inmates who worked in these arctic conditions had no winter clothing or adequate protection. Every day they were forced to work, even in icy driving rain and sleet, often without a break and continuously subjected to brutal treatment. Despite the conditions Höss was determined to get the prisoners to complete the main buildings by the end of the year no matter how it was done.

By early December work had forged ahead in spite of the harsh weather conditions. The wooden and barbed wire fence that had previously surrounded the camp had now been completely removed and replaced with a concrete one. The prefabricated guard towers too had been placed on order with a firm and were to arrive early the following year. The whole site, when completed, was to have a very large camp kitchen, utility, theatre, and registration buildings, Blockführer officer, commandant's office, camp administration offices, SS hospital, a fully operational crematorium, Gestapo offices, medical block, and a large water pool reserve for fire emergencies. It was also intended to have twenty-two two-storey buildings converted into prisoner quarters. Plans were drafted and approved for a prisoner hospital and offices and quarters for some of the camp's prisoners. The majority of these buildings were constructed in red brick, run in straight rows throughout the camp and were given block numbers for identification purposes. The Blockführer's guardhouse, however, was a wooden structure and this was built just outside the main gate. Another building under construction outside the main perimeter was a very large red brick building known as the registration building. Here new prisoners would be catalogued, receive their camp registration number and have their photograph taken, before being escorted by armed guard through the main gates to serve their sentence.

Most of the buildings that were built at Auschwitz and those planned for the future served merely to house and provide the basic needs for the prisoners, guards and SS staff that ran the camp. But there was one building constructed that symbolized the camp's culture, this was known as Block 13. It looked like any other red brick building that housed prisoners, but it had been chosen by the Political Department or Gestapo to be used purely for interrogating and torturing inmates with a variety of brutal and terrifying methods. In order to hold the prisoners for questioning, prison cells had been specially constructed in the basement.

January 1941 opened with a series of important deliberations for the staff at Auschwitz as it began to slowly enter a new crucial stage of its evolution. Although the bold plans envisaged from Berlin seemed encouraging for the successful continuation of the camp, the Economic and Administrative Office in Berlin begun putting forward new enterprising ideas for the camp. One of the ideas put forward was using Auschwitz's sand and gravel pits for the German Earth and Stone Works enterprise. This, it was envisaged, would ensure the future growth of the camp and as a consequence Auschwitz had to be enlarged purely to house a permanent slave labour population.

The significance of the plans meant that more prisoners were needed to be shipped to the camp quickly. Already there were around 8,000 Polish prisoners, and the list was growing daily. But the commandant was still far behind schedule with the building project and did not have adequate space or time to accommodate them properly. He was already seriously concerned about typhus and other infectious diseases breaking out. Conditions since early October were deplorable and he could see the situation getting much worse if he could not alleviate the problem of inadequate building supplies. Throughout January he worked tirelessly on the snow-covered camp trying to get the two-storey brick barracks completed so that they could meet the demands for the rapid expansion of the camp.

On 1 March 1941, SS-Reichsführer Heinrich Himmler and his large delegation arrived at Auschwitz and were given a guided tour of the camp. After the tour commandant Höss and Himmler with his delegation drove just outside the town of Auschwitz to a marshy tract of land in the Auschwitz district of Zasole, adjacent to the parent camp. Accompanied with maps and various architectural drawings of the land Himmler casually announced that the area they were standing on had been chosen as a new potential site. Auschwitz, he exclaimed, would be soon expanded, and here one day there would be a huge satellite camp constructed far greater than anything else planned or envisaged. This new camp, he said, would house a population of at least 100,000 prisoners.

Later Himmler spoke further about his grandiose ideas of transforming what he saw as the Auschwitz complex. In front of his Auschwitz staff he announced that he not only proposed to establish a huge satellite camp, but also intended to increase the Auschwitz camp population from the anticipated 10,000 inmates to 30,000. He made it clear that the massive increase in prisoner population was urgently required for labour availability, which was key to the progressive development of the region. The Reichsführer envisaged that gangs of slave labourers would be used to improve the dykes along the Sola and Vistula, and would also be put to work demolishing sites in the town for new building developments that were planned. In order to undertake these new building developments, he said, all Jewish and Polish residents living around the camp were to be evicted and incarcerated in a camp in the neighbourhood of Auschwitz and used as unskilled construction workers. By evicting these people it would allow the town to be available for the factory staff of a new massive enterprise that Himmler was eager to see built in the local area – IG Farben.

Officials from this massive chemical cartel had come to Auschwitz with Himmler to decide finally whether a factory should be built in the area. For some time I.G Farben had shown interest in the region around Auschwitz, and particularly welcomed using large numbers of skilled and unskilled construction workers from the concentration camps. It was estimated that between 8,000 and 12,000 men would be required to construct the factory, and with the Reichsführer's new plans to increase the pool of prisoners at Auschwitz to 30,000, he had more than enough. By expanding Auschwitz he not only provided IG Farben with adequate amounts of slave labour, but could commit 10,000 inmates to his planned agricultural estate as well.

The Reichsführer's audacious plans of turning Auschwitz into a huge agricultural experimental centre were still very much a fundamental part of his overall vision. He also made it known he had no intention of giving up the plans for the gravel and sand pit enterprises either. He tried his best to assure the commandant that the enterprises would be good for the region, and it could not be made possible without expanding and developing Auschwitz. It was for this reason, he said, that IG Farben had to be given the highest priority. A site had already been chosen for a factory about 2 miles away. It would be built to produce synthetic rubber, called Buna, and inmates from Auschwitz were to help construct it. Other construction workers too from Germany would be brought in and be accommodated in vacant homes in Auschwitz town. The town itself would be redeveloped and schools and hospitals built purely for the German workers. Himmler also announced to the commandant that he intended to move some of the arms industry into the area as well.

On 27 March, Höss and his Auschwitz officials and company representatives of IG Farben held a meeting to speak about the company's involvement and the advantages that it would bring by working together. By early April construction work finally begun on the new Buna factory. Without delay gangs of prison workers from Auschwitz were sent to the village of Monowitz on foot every morning to commence their shift building the new IG Farben plant. Already plans were being drawn up and approved to construct additional quarters for the inmates and to build a bridge over the Sola to connect the camp and the factory. A narrow-gauge railway line too was considered so that the inmates could be quickly transported to the plant.

This new enterprise was of giant proportions, but true to the Reichsführer's word, extensive assistance from Auschwitz's slave labour population ensured its rapid creation. Almost as soon as building work commenced, the relationship between the SS and IG Farben thrived with both parties enthusiastically planning to develop a new dominion befitting the SS. In fact, the Auschwitz camp too had been incorporated in this new masterplan with architects designing a general plan for its expansion.

As a result of this expansion a new chief of Office II of the SS Main Office House-hold and Buildings, Hans Kammler, headed the expansion plans of the Auschwitz complex. In the plans it was proposed there would be the immediate construction of thirty new two-storey barracks, which were to be extended towards the station, housing for the commandant's staff and for officers, a delousing facility, a laundry, a storehouse for prisoners' belongings, and even a large roll call area flanked by an entrance pavilion. Among other things there were plans for a camp for civilian employees and construction workers. New streets would be built with an extensive new drainage and sewer system including a drinking water installation. There were also plans for an SS private railway station, an SS settlement and – one of Himmler's largest ideas – the massive agricultural project, which included the building of new villages, farmsteads and the construction of an agricultural estate with barns and giant greenhouses.

In the main Auschwitz camp one particular part of the camp that was outlined was an area behind the camp prison near to the hospital and close to a newly designed crematorium. Architects had chosen this area, with its own execution yard in the centre. It was proposed that both the camp authorities and the Gestapo would use this area in a similar manner to the way executions were conducted at Block 11, but with a difference. According to the plan the condemned would be taken straight to this execution yard, stripped naked, executed and their corpses carried immediately into the crematorium to be incinerated. The idea seemed perfect, but even Himmler wanted the plans changed, outlining that it would be more practical and efficient to run the new and old crematoria side-by-side, and close to the back gate of the camp. In this way he was sure that Auschwitz could handle larger groups of victims. He made it known that permanent crematoria, incinerating sites, and execution grounds of various designs were being installed elsewhere at a number of concentration camps. Therefore he felt it was very important to discuss with the commandant these execution facilities at Auschwitz and possibilities to make them even more sophisticated. He went on to tell Höss that the killings would be undertaken with the slightest amount of disorder and disturbance. According to the '14f13' programme guidelines, all those regarded to be chronically sick, mentally ill, and invalid inmates who were Jewish, were now automatically to be selected for immediate removal from camp life.

Since September 1940 the Auschwitz crematorium had been working at a steady pace burning the bodies of prisoners who had died of natural causes or had been killed or executed. Within weeks of it going into operation it was estimated that six bodies were being burnt every hour. This number soon doubled, and by 1941 the crematorium had reached its maximum capacity of eighteen bodies per hour. In direct response to the dramatic increase of deaths in the camp Höss was prompted to authorise the expansion of the crematorium and approached the SS New Construction Office with an urgent request for a second double-muffle incinerator. The second incinerator was fitted at a reduced cost owing to the fact that it was attached to the ventilator of the first. With the new second double-muffle incinerator the rate of cremation doubled, but still more and more people were found to liquidate. In the summer heat the stench was foul that the camp's architect, Schlachter, installed a more sophisticated ventilation system so it could not only extract the bad odours but also provide a fresh supply of air from outside the building.

During the morning of 22 June Höss received news that a massive assemblage of more than 3 million German troops had attacked the Soviet Union and were victoriously forging ahead. In Höss's eyes Russia was a land ripe for plunder. He was firmly convinced that the Russians were an inferior race and had come to appreciate the Nazi theory of the connection between Communism and Judaism. Within days he was told about ruthless actions against Russian Jews, Communist politicians and political commissars. Although Auschwitz remained a camp primarily for Polish prisoners, he received reports that the SS were actually weeding out commissars that were found hiding in German army PoW camps. The first of these Soviet prisoners were transported to Auschwitz in July. Several hundred of them were marched through the main gate and from the moment they arrived they were treated much worse than the Polish inmates. They were hated at Auschwitz. Many of them were beaten and tortured, while some were shot in the gravel pits or were condemned to the cellars of Block 11. Here they were locked in the dark cold cells and left to starve to death.

As a result of these increased deaths at Auschwitz the crematorium was once again working to full capacity. Executions were now so frequent that Höss was compelled to discuss at his meetings a more effective method of killing than just starving, shooting and hanging the victims, or having them murdered by lethal injection. He told his staff that to find an effective method was essential to guarantee the rapid effectiveness of cleansing the camp of what he deemed were undesirables, and those unfit for work.

Höss already knew, as did his closest associates, of the euthanasia programme. In fact, the 14f13 programme had already reached Auschwitz with effective results. Inmates had been removed from the camp and transported to special killing centres in Germany, where vans had been converted into mobile gas chambers built to look like shower rooms. The sick, chronically ill or physically disabled were sent to the compartment of a converted van, the airtight doors were then slammed shut, and the victims inside were asphyxiated by bottled carbon monoxide. Both Höss and his deputy, Fritzsch, thought the idea of asphyxiation was probably the most effective means of homicide. It was thus proposed that they considered it further as a killing process at Auschwitz.

As Höss and Fritzsch pondered on ways of killing by asphyxiation, in late August SS-Obersturmbannführer Adolf Eichmann travelled from the RSHA in Berlin to meet with the commandant at Auschwitz. Eichmann was a Jewish emigration specialist who had been given the task of facilitating and managing the logistics of mass deportations of Jews to ghettos and concentration camps in Nazi-occupied Eastern Europe. He had been sent specifically to Auschwitz to discuss new deportation plans and to look at the camp's facilities. Eichmann made it clear that Himmler wanted the Jewish question solved once and for all, and it was the SS that was to implement that order. Preparations for the mass deportation of Jews were now going to take place, and with the excellent railway network to Auschwitz coupled with the expansion programme of the camp, it was considered the most viable location to which to transport Jews. He made it quite clear that Himmler envisaged Auschwitz as the main hub of a huge semi-industrial complex. Here the transports would arrive and then selected Jews would be sent to work at one of the many sub-camps being built nearby. Then, when they were no longer required or deemed unfit for work, they could be transported the few miles back to the camp, and exterminated. But for now the area was still not regarded as a viable transit point, so it was agreed that the Jews would have to remain in the ghettos until Auschwitz was prepared ready for them.

Another important question on Eichmann's list was the design of an improved killing facility at the camp which would be capable of exterminating larger numbers of inmates. Since early summer Höss had been aware of growing plans to systematically murder prisoners at Auschwitz. Initially the condemned had just been the sick and disabled, now Eichmann announced that Himmler had decided about grander plans of producing a factory-like killing installation that was capable of removing anyone deemed a threat to the Reich or unfit for slave labour. Russian PoWs were regarded as subhuman and on the Reichsführer's agenda for liquidation, and it was suggested that it would be practical to use the Russian PoWs in a killing experiment. It was agreed that carbon monoxide chambers used in the mobile gas chamber vans were far too expensive. Instead, Höss proposed using hydrogen cyanide and to construct a delousing installation at Auschwitz where he could perhaps use a lethal substance made up of hydrogen cyanide.

On 3 September, an experiment was undertaken to gas Russian PoWs using crystallized prussic acid, which was sold in tins marked under the name of Zyklon B. The basement of Block 11 was used for the gassing. Windows and other areas of the basement were made airtight before removing the condemned from their sickbeds and hovels. Under the cover of darkness they were escorted down to Block 11 where they were herded tightly into the underground cells. Zyklon B crystals were then thrown into the room where Russian prisoners and the sick inmates were standing. Although many of them were asphyxiated within twenty minutes of the gassing, some prisoners did in fact survive the ordeal, and had to be shot.

While it was deemed the gassing experiment was a success it was agreed that the basement was not ideal for use as a gas chamber. A solution was soon found in using the camp's crematorium. It not only had a flat roof, but could easily be adapted with various openings in order to allow the Zyklon B crystals to be poured in. The new powerful ventilation system that had just been fitted in the morgue would be more than capable of dealing with the poisonous gas.

Almost immediately men were set to work to modify the crematorium into a gas chamber. On the flat roof three square portholes were made through the morgue roof and covered with wooden lids. It was through these portholes that the Zyklon B crystals were to be poured.

Once the crematorium had been prepared for a mass killing experiment, 900 Russian soldiers were chosen to be gassed. The gassing of the Soviet soldiers took place on 16 September. Prior to the gassing, an area around the crematorium was sealed off and it was forbidden to look at the roof of the crematorium, which was visible from the windows of the SS hospital on the first floor. The crematorium forecourt too was closed off to all prisoners working in the camp for it was being utilised as an undressing area for the victims. First the victims were ordered to undress and then they were herded naked into the morgue where they were gassed with Zyklon B crystals. Auschwitz had now finally evolved into an efficient killing machine using a tried and tested gassing procedure. The success of this murder factory now depended on how its facilities were going to cope with the growing influx of prisoners that were sent to their deaths.

(*This and the following 3 pages*) A series of photographs taken on three different visits over three years to the site showing the entrance to the main Auschwitz complex, known as Auschwitz I. During May or June 1940 this entrance had a new steel gate fitted. Along the top of the gate's frame the inscription reads '*Arbeit Macht Frei*' – 'Work Makes You Free'. In the mind of the Nazis, all prisoners that entered through these gates were enemies of the state and their punishment through forced labour was justified. (*HITM archive & Auschwitz-Birkenau Museum*)

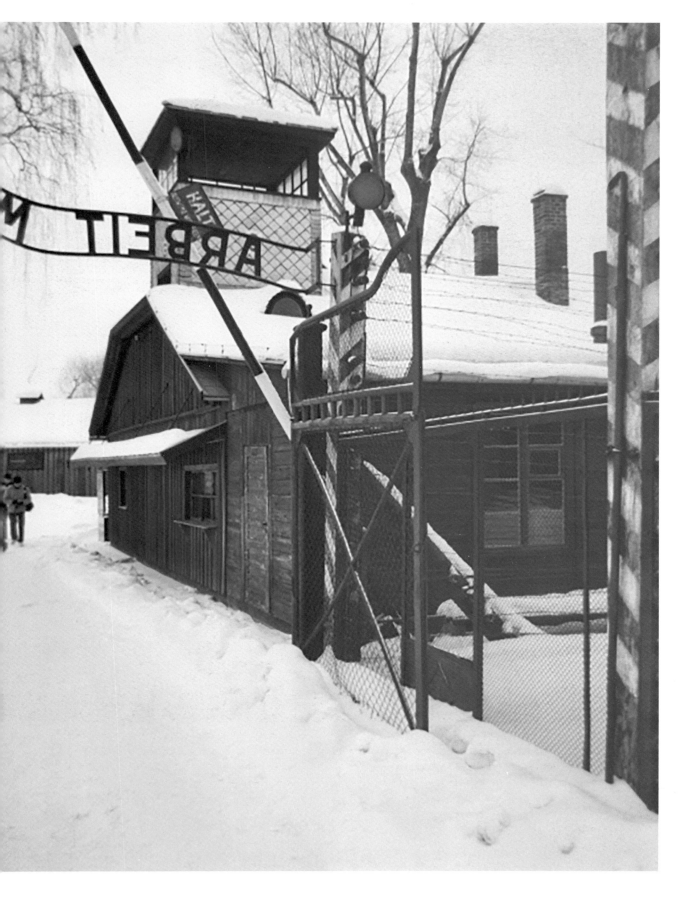

(*Above and the following page*) Three photographs taken in the depths of the winter of January 2006 showing the administration and commandant's office buildings. Further along the thoroughfare at the bottom of the camp to the left was the commandant's house, better known as the Höss Villa. It can just be seen, concealed by trees. (*HITM archive & Auschwitz-Birkenau Museum*)

(*Opposite above*) A photograph taken in the snow in 2006 looking across from near the entrance to the camp showing the doubled barbed wire electric fenced area and beyond. Beyond the fenced area to the right with the many chimneys are the camp's kitchens. Next to that building is the post office barracks and then the prisoners' infirmary block. (*HITM archive & Auschwitz-Birkenau Museum*)

(*Opposite below*) A photograph of the former commandant's office, Rudolf Höss, at Auschwitz. I. This large, imposing building generally handled matters concerning SS staff. All records were stored here, as well as weapons and other important military equipment. Transport and communication matters were also controlled from this headquarters. The office was divided into a number of different sections: office supplies, communications office, judicial affairs, weapons, military supplies, and the engineer's office. Rudolf Höss had his own personal office, as well as a boardroom where he and his staff gathered twice a week. (*HITM archive & Auschwitz-Birkenau Museum*)

On the right of the doubled barbed wire electric fence is a prisoners' block house which was used as a Russian PoW camp between October 1941 and March 1942. On the left are the administration and commandant's office buildings. Note the two wooden watch towers, one between two buildings and the other erected on the perimeter of the camp. A sign reads 'Beware High Tension Electric Fence, Danger to Life'. *(HITM archive & Auschwitz-Birkenau Museum)*

The same photograph as the previous one but taken in the snow in January 2006 showing the prisoners' block houses and the administration and commandant's office buildings. *(HITM archive & Auschwitz-Birkenau Museum)*

(*Above*) A photograph taken in the snow in 2006 looking across from near the entrance to the camp showing the doubled barbed wire electric fenced area and beyond. Beyond the fenced area to the left is the post office barracks and then the prisoners' infirmary block. (*HITM archive & Auschwitz-Birkenau Museum*)

(*Opposite above*) One of a number of signs posted around the camp warning prisoners not to pass beyond the sign into a prohibited stretch of land bordering the high tension electric fence. The red brick building in front of the fence is the registration building. Here new prisoners would be catalogued, receive their camp registration number, and have their photograph taken before being escorted by armed guard through the main gates to serve their sentence. (*HITM archive & Auschwitz-Birkenau Museum*)

(*Opposite below*) A photograph taken looking down towards the prisoners quarters, Block 25. On the right of the electric fence is the former registration building, and on the left is the camp kitchen. Note two of the camp's prefabricated guard towers on the right. These were erected in early 1941. The whole site, when completed, was to have a very large camp kitchen, a utility building, a theatre, registration buildings, Blockführer office, commandant's office, camp administration offices, SS hospital, a fully operational crematorium, Gestapo offices, medical block, and a large water pool reserve for fire emergencies. (*HITM archive & Auschwitz-Birkenau Museum*)

Near the entrance of the camp in front of a building where the inmates once played music in the camp's orchestra. Classical music was often played here as the prisoners marched in and out of the camp.

A photograph taken during the camp's operation in a Sunday concert in 1941, where SS men also attended with the prisoners. The orchestra was conducted by Franciszek Nierychlo. (*USHMM, courtesy of Instytut Pamieci Narodowej*)

A photograph of the SS sick bay. The camp's crematorium and gas chamber can just be seen behind this building at the far end. *(HITM archive & Auschwitz-Birkenau Museum)*

To the left of the prefabricated wooden guard tower is the SS hospital building. This building overlooked the camp's crematorium, which can be identified by the tall brick-built chimney. In the summer of 1940 this building was primarily to function as a crematorium but it would also serve for prisoner delousing. Before the crematorium came into operation, those who died at the camp were transported to Gliwice and incinerated in the municipal crematorium. The conversion of the crematorium was undertaken with the authorisation of the SS Construction Management. *(HITM archive & Auschwitz-Birkenau Museum)*

(*Above*) Another photograph looking from the side of the SS sick bay building. Looking down, the entrance of the camp can just be seen on the far right. Beyond that, the large red building just outside the camp compound is the registration building. (*HITM archive & Auschwitz-Birkenau Museum*)

(*Opposite above*) Looking along, with the prisoner blocks either side down to the bottom where there is a pre-fabricated wooden watch tower, is the admission building. (*HITM archive & Auschwitz-Birkenau Museum*)

(*Opposite below*) Prisoner blocks either side looking down to the prefabricated wooden watch tower beyond, where the perimeter of the camp can just be seen, comprising of a concrete wall, topped with barbed wire. (*HITM archive & Auschwitz-Birkenau Museum*)

(*Above*) Looking down towards the concrete perimeter fence. On the left are prisoner Blocks 14 and 3. On the right are prisoner Blocks 15 and 4. Initially when the camp first opened in mid-1940, it was intended to have twenty-two two-storey buildings converted into prisoner quarters. Plans were drafted and approved for a prisoner hospital and offices and quarters for some of the camp's prisoners. The majority of these buildings were constructed in red brick, run in straight rows throughout the camp, and were given block numbers for identification purposes. (*HITM archive & Auschwitz-Birkenau Museum*)

(*Opposite above*) A photograph showing a sentry box and to the left of it a gallows in front of the brick kitchen building. On 19 July 1943 there was a hanging of twelve Polish political prisoners here in a reprisal for the escape of three prisoners. The gallows were not high enough for the prisoners and they died an agonizing death. (*HITM archive & Auschwitz-Birkenau Museum*)

(*Opposite below*) On the left is Block 24. This is where the prisoners had the camp brothel. The directive for a camp brothel came from Himmler, who thought it would be an incentive to promote a hard work ethic. It was also a good probability that in the minds of the SS the establishment of a brothel would stop homosexuality within the camp, and this included forcing homosexuals into the brothel in order to cure them. (*HITM archive & Auschwitz-Birkenau Museum*)

(*Above*) A photograph showing the camp kitchen on the left and the admission building on the right. (*HITM archive & Auschwitz-Birkenau Museum*)

(*Opposite above*) One of a number of signs posted around the camp warning prisoners not to pass beyond the sign into a prohibited stretch of land bordering the high tension electric fence. The red brick building in front of the fence is the registration building. Here new prisoners would be catalogued, receive their camp registration number and have their photograph taken, before being escorted by armed guard through the main gates to serve their sentence. (*HITM archive & Auschwitz-Birkenau Museum*)

(*Opposite below*) A locked gate which could be entered by prisoners under armed supervision. This area separated the main camp by the registration building on the right by the double high tension electric fence. On the left are the camp kitchens. (*HITM archive & Auschwitz-Birkenau Museum*)

(*Above*) Looking across to the right is the double high tension electric fence, and beyond is the perimeter of the camp comprising of a high concrete wall topped with barbed wire. In the distance just beyond the wooden watch tower is the commandant's house, known as the Höss villa between 1940 and 1944. (*HITM archive & Auschwitz-Birkenau Museum*)

(*Opposite above*) A closer photograph showing part of the high concrete wall topped with barbed wire. This photograph was taken at the corner perimeter of the camp and shows part of the roof of the Höss villa. (*HITM archive & Auschwitz-Birkenau Museum*)

(*Opposite below*) On the left are prisoner Blocks 1, 12 and 22. On the right between the high tension electric fence is the commandant's office, camp administration offices and the SS hospital. In 1940 most of the buildings that were built at Auschwitz and those planned for the future served merely to house and provide the basic needs of the prisoners, guards and SS staff that ran the camp. (*HITM archive & Auschwitz-Birkenau Museum*)

A photograph taken along a path enclosed by a high tension electric fence. Either side are red brick block houses, Blocks 1, 12 and 22, with the commandant's office, camp administration offices and the SS hospital. At the end you can just see one of the wooden watch towers. (*HITM archive & Auschwitz-Birkenau Museum*)

In the snow, Blocks 24, 23 and 22 can be seen on the left. On the right are Blocks 14, 13 and 12. These comprised of the old Russian PoW camp between 1941 and 1942. At the end, just beyond the double high tension electric fence either side of the prefabricated wooden watch tower, is the SS sick bay on the left and administration building on the right. (*HITM archive & Auschwitz-Birkenau Museum*)

A photograph showing how the camp looked during the war from a slightly closer view of the wooden watch tower in the previous photograph. (*USHMM, courtesy of Instytut Pamieci Narodowej*)

(*This and the following 3 pages*) A series of photographs taken in sequence showing the commandant Rudolf Höss's former family residence as it stands today. They were taken in February 2007. Kevin Bowden and tour guide Halina Kapka, pictured here, both accompanied the author during his research of the Höss villa and complex. Right of the house is the garden, while on the left is the private entrance used by Höss. The Höss villa was an imposing two-storey stucco building situated in the north-eastern corner of the camp. (*HITM archive & Auschwitz-Birkenau Museum*)

(*This and the following 7 pages*) A series of photographs taken in sequence showing the gardens surrounding the Höss villa. At the side of the building the house was reached by a concrete path and a flight of concrete steps leading to the side door with a porch and overlooking the garden. The garden itself was predominantly situated to the side of the house and consisted of a number of trees and shrubberies from the previous occupants. A normal fence was initially erected around the perimeter of the garden and the house in order to divide it from the main camp. In November 1940 a new high concrete fencing was constructed topped with barbed wire to replace the old fencing around the entire boundary of the camp. The new fencing was also installed at the rear and the sides of the Höss villa, making the house completely separated from the camp. The camp was virtually invisible from the garden, except for the roofs and chimneys of the commandant's office and the administration buildings. The fence to the rear of the house, which hid the commandant's office, administration offices, SS guardhouse and the newly constructed crematorium, was further hidden by a large mound of earth placed behind the fence, and trees planted. Höss had been particularly insistent on trying to conceal the villa from the camp as much as possible, and made it known that he wanted his family to live in absolute privacy. (*HITM archive & Auschwitz-Birkenau Museum*)

A very rare group of four photographs taken from an attic window show the rear of the Höss villa in February 2007, overlooking the commandant's office, administration building and the SS sick bay. Note the trees planted in front of the concrete wall in an attempt to conceal the camp from the house. (*HITM archive & Auschwitz-Birkenau Museum*)

Two photographs taken from the same bedroom but a different window overlooking the side of the house. They show part of the concrete fenced garden, beyond this the prefabricated wooden watch tower, and Blocks 1–7. (*HITM archive & Auschwitz-Birkenau Museum*)

Two photographs showing the cellar of the Höss villa.
(*HITM archive & Auschwitz-Birkenau Museum*)

A photograph taken in January 2006 showing the Höss villa in the distance. The buildings on the right comprise the SS sick bay, administration building and commandant's office. (*HITM archive & Auschwitz-Birkenau Museum*)

The following six photographs were taken from some of the rooms of the Höss villa in February 2007. According to Aniela Bednarska, who was one of the housekeepers in the Höss villa at the time, the plan of the house consisted of a living room, which comprised of 'black furniture, a sofa, two armchairs, a table, two stools, and a standing lamp. There was Höss's study, which you could enter either from the living room or the dining room. The room was furnished with a big desk covered with a transparent plastic board under which he kept family pictures, two leather armchairs, a long narrow bookcase covering two walls and filled with books. One of its sections was locked. Höss kept cigarettes and vodka there. The furniture was matt nut-brown, made by camp prisoners. The dining room was decorated with dark nut-brown furniture made in the camp, an unfolding table, six leather chairs, a glazed cupboard for glassware, a sideboard and a beautiful plant stand. The furniture was solid and tasteful. The parquet floor was covered with beautiful and expensive carpets, different colours in every room. There were beautiful curtains in the windows. The kitchen had white walls with white tiles, a big white cupboard where dishes were kept, a small cupboard for papers and brushes, and two white stools. There were three taps with running water for washing up. Next to the kitchen was the pantry. This was very well stocked and open … all the groceries were brought by the prisoners … The bathroom downstairs had white tiles, while upstairs it had light green. The main hall had a hanger with a mirror covering the whole wall. From this hall there were stone stairs leading upstairs to four rooms. The first room was Mr and Mrs Höss's bedroom. The room had two dark nut-brown beds, a four-winged wardrobe made in the camp and used by Höss, a lighter wardrobe with glass doors used by Mrs Höss. There was also a sort of couch – hollowed and leather. Above the beds there was a big colourful oil painting depicting a bunch of field flowers. There were tile stoves in the rooms. Radiators were installed at the end of 1941 and they were hidden behind wooden boxes the same colour as the furniture. In the next room, above Höss's study was the children's bedroom. The furniture was light and made with a bed net, a big light nut-brown wardrobe, a table, a chest of drawers and cream-coloured chairs. Above the kitchen and the pantry there was a separate room intended for the children to study and play. There was a dark table, hard chairs, a big wide blue couch and a large stand for books and toys. There was an enormous amount of toys in the room. The separate room above the black one was a guest room. There were two dark beds, a wardrobe and a set of shelves. All the walls were covered with light beige wallpaper with leaves of a darker shade … There were three basements and in one of them there was a laundry room. In the passageway there were two high water boilers … In the house I did all the housework – cleaning, laundering, ironing, cooking, and dishwashing.' To decorate the villa walls with pictures, Höss ordered the prisoner Mieczysław Kościelniak who was a renowned Polish artist to come to the house and sort and select the best art collections that the commandant had gathered at his home. According to Kościelniak the art works had been taken from demolished Polish homes during the construction of the camp. (*HITM archive & Auschwitz-Birkenau Museum*)

In its present state two photographs showing the northwest side of Crematorium I in the Auschwitz main camp. In September 1944 the crematorium was shut down, its chimney removed, and it was converted into an air raid shelter for the SS hospital. The chimney was re-built in 1946/7. Note the steel-faced, gas-tight door with peephole. (*HITM archive & Auschwitz-Birkenau Museum*)

One of the ovens in Crematorium I at Auschwitz main camp taken in November 2008. This crematorium operated from August 1940 until the summer of 1943. According to German records, some 340 corpses could be burned every twenty-four hours after the installation of the three furnaces. (*HITM archive & Auschwitz-Birkenau Museum*)

Here stands the gallows where Commandant Rudolf Höss was hanged in April 1947.

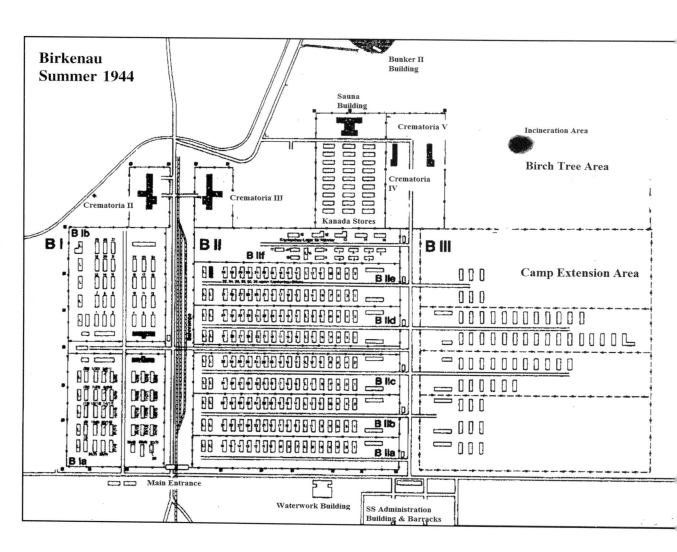

Birkenau
Summer 1944

Bunker II
Building

Sauna
Building

Crematoria V

Incineration Area

Birch Tree Area

Crematoria
IV

Crematoria II

Crematoria III

Kanada Stores

B I   B Ib

B II

B IIf

B III

Camp Extension Area

B IIe

B IId

B IIc

B IIb

B Ia   B IIa

Main Entrance

Waterwork Building

SS Administration
Building & Barracks

Phase II

Birkenau

(Death & Labour Camp)

Although the improved killing facility at Auschwitz had more or less been achieved with the use of Zyklon B crystals, Höss had become increasingly concerned at the amount of Russian PoWs that would be sent to the camp and pass through the crematorium. By September he had received news that the Germans had already captured an estimated 3 million Soviet prisoners. Some 100,000 of them were transferred from the Army to the SS in September, and many were earmarked for Auschwitz. According to a report, Himmler had ordered Hans Kammler to inform the commandant of Auschwitz that the long-awaited giant PoW camp at Auschwitz would be constructed next to the parent camp. Its construction was to house many of the new Soviet PoWs and the environment in which they were to be placed would ensure that large numbers of them would perish.

The site chosen for the extension of Auschwitz was near the Polish village of Brzezinka. This marshy tract of land surrounded by birch woods was situated nearly 2 miles west of the main camp. Although there had never been any concrete plans to construct a massive PoW camp on the land, as a precaution the houses of the small village of Brzezinka were cleared by the SS in July and all its inhabitants relocated elsewhere. The Germans renamed the area Birkenau.

The task of designing Birkenau was left in the capable hands of the newly appointed chief of the Auschwitz construction office SS-Hauptsturmführer Karl Bischoff, and the 33-year-old architect SS-Rottenführer Fritz Ertl. The total budget for the construction was to be 8.9 million Reich Marks. The projected number of prisoners to be housed in the camp was 97,000. It was planned that Birkenau would be divided into a two-part camp, with the smaller part of only 17,000 inmates located in a quarantine camp. The accommodation was to be very overcrowded and initial plans were for one barrack block to contain 550 inmates. This amount was soon altered to a final figure of 744.

In the quarantine camp it was planned that there were going to be two delousing stations, two kitchens, thirty barracks each accommodating 744 men, five toilet barracks, and five washrooms. In the main part of the installation, the camp was to be divided into twelve camps, each with twelve barracks, one kitchen, one toilet barracks, and one washroom. All inmates were to be housed in 174 barracks, each barrack subdivided into sixty-two bays, and each bay having a three bunk-bed system.

The size of the construction was to be on a scale that not even Höss could have envisaged. The whole area covered over eighty hectares. On a couple of occasions he actually visited the location on his own in order to try to formulate an impression in his mind on the sheer size of the area of land upon which the new satellite camp would be built. Following the example of the main camp, Höss had been entrusted with selecting inmates to build the Birkenau site. With so many Russian PoWs in captivity, he was ordered to use the vast pool of prisoners offered from the German Army. Höss received confirmation from Himmler's office that the Russian PoWs would be used for slave labour to build the new camp.

In early October, Höss finally authorised the transportation order of his new Russian labour force. In total 10,000 Russian prisoners from Lamsdorf were to be marched to Auschwitz. The journey to the camp was one of complete horror.

Almost as soon as the Russian PoWs arrived in Auschwitz they were ordered to work. Those that were too weak were killed and disposed of in the crematorium, while the remaining prisoners were dragged from their barracks and marched the forty minutes to the Birkenau construction site. The first job was to dismantle the existing village and then start building the camp. The Russians had not been given any tools with which to demolish the houses. Instead they were required to pull down the buildings with their bare hands. The physical condition of the men was appalling, but they were still forced to work. All day long they laboured in freezing temperatures. First they had to level the ground, then drainage ditches had to be dug, and then finally the various brick barracks and prefabricated wooden horse stables had to be constructed. The speed of the work was of utmost importance, and within fourteen days the quarantine camp had been completed.

Throughout the building project at Birkenau, Höss was constantly updated with its progress. Regularly he was seen visiting the construction site, either by motor vehicle or on horseback. On numerous occasions he could be seen wandering around the building site discussing details of the construction programme with site managers and subordinates. He soon discovered, which came as no surprise, that the labour force had not been supplied with adequate building materials. Consequently the barracks had to be built from brick, as there were dwindling supplies of wood. Most of the building materials during October and November were taken from the demolition of the hamlet of Birkenau, but still this did not meet the requirements of Bischoff. The mortality rate too was also considered a problem; by the end of October 1,255 Soviet prisoners had died. News of the high death rate concerned SS head-quarters in Berlin for they looked upon the prisoners as an asset.

Despite this, the death rate continued to rise. Many inmates were dying of starvation, illness, injuries, and being subjected to more or less unrestrained killing. Höss recalled that Soviet prisoners died more rapidly than he ever expected. According to him the situation became much worse during the muddy period of the winter of 1941. With the increased fatality rate the crematorium in Auschwitz was once again approaching its maximum incineration capacity. Höss was informed through discussions with Grabner and Schlachter that the existing crematorium just could not cope with the large numbers of prisoners. The crematorium was not built for an inmate population of 10,000, and with the influx of Russian prisoners, it was agreed that it could not possibly service the PoWs as well. Bischoff immediately summoned the Topf engineer Kurt Prüfer who had supplied the main incineration equipment to Auschwitz. He arrived in the camp on Tuesday, 21 October, to go over plans, suggesting that the crematorium combine three muffles in a single furnace. In their view it was deemed impractical to waste money building a crematorium on the new Birkenau site, as the camp promised to be only a temporary solution until the war in Russia was won. Therefore it was agreed that a new crematorium could perhaps be built in the main camp near the administration building and alongside the existing crematorium.

Over the ensuing weeks, construction of the Birkenau site continued. Bischoff informed Berlin that in spite of the increased death rate among the Soviet prisoners, much work had been achieved at Birkenau. In fact, according to reports, Bischoff confirmed that in just over one month 140,000 cubic feet of earth had been excavated, 1,600 concrete foundations laid, 600 concrete posts erected for the fence with 100,000 feet of barbed wire, and 86,000 cubic feet of brickwork had been constructed, using more than 1 million bricks. Constructing the actual barracks, however, was still a slow process. Much of the construction of the barracks was to be built from wood. A German company had already designed the standard army horse stable barrack, and this would be produced and dispatched to Auschwitz as a kit, where it could easily be erected and dismantled. It was argued that these prefabricated wooden huts could be assembled very rapidly with a gang of just thirty unskilled men led by one carpenter. In total 253 of these huts were assigned to Birkenau.

By the end of 1941, Auschwitz was slowly transformed from a quiet backwater quarantine camp in south western Poland, into one of the largest concentration camp systems of the Reich. In little over a year Auschwitz had developed into a dual function camp with the inmates that were sent there now living and working. They were also dying. With an effective killing facility mastered, more and more undesirables of the Reich could be given passage through the infamous *Arbeit Macht Frei* gates.

On Thursday, 27 February, Höss, SS architect Bischoff and Kammler, head of the Central SS Building Office, held a meeting to discuss their concerns about constructing another crematorium at the base camp, or what was now being formally called Auschwitz I. During the meeting it was agreed that they would abandon the idea of another crematorium at Auschwitz I and move the location to the new camp at Birkenau. Plans for the new crematorium had already been drawn up the previous October and it was expected to arrive very soon. Poring over plans of the Birkenau site Höss announced that he had personally visited the camp to find the perfect location for a killing installation. Scouring the far north western corner of the camp he had found an abandoned small brick cottage with a tiled roof. He decided that the cottage, known as Bunker I and nicknamed 'the little red house', should be converted as quickly as possible. As part of the conversion, its windows and doors were to be bricked up, its edges sealed with felt in order to ensure it was airtight, and the interior gutted to form two rooms. The doors to both rooms were to have a sign attached over the entrances: '*Zur Desinfektion*' ('To Disinfection'). Those unfit for work could be taken away with ease and gassed in secrecy, and their death cries would not disturb the local surroundings. This new killing facility at Bunker I was to be similar to that of the main camp, but on a grander scale.

Bunker I was completed within a few weeks and on 20 March was made operational for the first time. Soon after its completion a communication from the RSHA in Berlin sent a telegram outlining that a group of Jews unfit for work from Upper Silesia had been chosen locally for what the SS authorities were now calling 'special treatment'. Under the cover of darkness the Jews were transported direct to Birkenau.

Throughout the spring and summer, Bunker I, together with Crematorium I in the main camp, continued to carry out the killing of convicted criminals and those unfit for work. During early June in spite of the increased numbers going to their death Höss was still not happy with its efficiency. In order to facilitate the transports arriving at the camp he held a meeting with SS-Sturmbannführer Karl Bischoff and other members of the Auschwitz Construction Office to discuss plans to convert a second cottage known as the 'Little White House' into what he called a 'bathing facility for special actions'. By the end of June this quiet and unobtrusive looking house, known as Bunker II, went into operation. The interior of the cottage comprised four narrow rooms that were constructed as gas chambers. With better ventilation and a killing capacity of around 1,200 people at any one time, Höss was sure that Birkenau would run efficiently as never before.

As the last finishing touches were made to Bunker II more shipments of Jews were destined for Auschwitz. The killing methods were efficient, but the SS were faced with a growing problem of disposing of the bodies from Bunkers I and II. From the gas chamber entrance the corpses would be loaded onto a truck and driven to a pit and dumped. Powdered lime would be thrown over the bodies and then covered with soil. However, some 107,000 corpses had been buried in Birkenau and were now decomposing and as a consequence were polluting the ground water. It was ordered that these corpses be dug up and burned on specially constructed grills.

But this type of cremation was far from efficient, and plans were drawn up to transform the murder and disposal of the inmates. It had been planned to enlarge the capacity of the Birkenau site to 200,000 inmates. Karl Bischoff had drawn up a plan for the Birkenau site to include two crematoria, numbered II and III. The crematorium at the main camp was renamed Crematorium I. Another crematorium, known as Crematorium IV, was sketched in next to Bunker I, and Crematorium V next to Bunker II. It was estimated that each crematorium had an incineration capacity of 576 corpses a day. In Höss's eyes, this appeared more than enough to deal with the high volumes that were pouring into the camp. From inception both Crematorium IV and V were to operate as killing centres. They would have their own gas chambers, morgue, and a furnace hall. The other crematoria would also be transformed to operate as killing machines. Birkenau, it seemed, had finally evolved and was now developing into a factory of death.

In total eleven construction companies were involved in the building of all the crematoria. The civilian firm called Huta, from Kattowitz, was already working on the shell of Crematorium II, and then began work on Wednesday, 23 September, on Crematorium IV. A total of about eighty men worked on the site; sixty or so were prisoners, of which twenty worked for the Auschwitz contractor Koehler on building the chimneys. In total between 100 and 150 persons, of whom the majority were prisoners, were employed on the individual work sites. In order to ensure all the firms worked well together, a Sonderführer would manage the works in progress and see that the job was completed efficiently and as quickly as possible. For the ensuing weeks and months to come he oversaw firms like Karl Falck from Gleiwitz and the Triton Company from Kattowitz that handled the drainage work of Crematoria III, IV and V. The Klug Company from Gleiwitz helped Topf and Sons build the furnaces of Crematorium IV and V. Huta were contracted to complete the floor and walls of the two underground morgues of Crematorium II, while the Vedag Company from Breslau, were paid to waterproof the cellars of Crematoria II and III.

At the end of January 1943, Engineer Kurt Prüfer of Topf and Sons inspected the work sites 30, 30a, 30b, and 30c and reported that 'Crematorium II was structurally completed except for minor secondary work. The three-muffle cremation furnaces are ready and at present are being dry heated. The delivery of the ventilation unit for the corpse cellar was delayed as a result of the suspension on railway cars, so that the installation can take place sooner than ten days from now. Therefore, the start of operation of Crematorium II will probably be ready by 15 February 1943.' But despite Prüfer's confidence the construction had in fact fallen behind by two months. In the first half of February, Erfurt received a letter from Topf & Sons regarding an order for Crematorium III. It read: 'We once again confirm receipt of your order for five triple muffle furnaces, including two electric lifts for the corpses and one provisional hoist for corpses. Also the order for a practical device for charging coal and a device for transporting ashes. You are to deliver the whole installation for Crematorium III. We expect you to take the necessary steps to immediately dispatch all machines and parts. The complete installation must come into service on 10 April 1943.'

At the end of February Höss received encouraging words that the five triple-muffle furnaces in Crematorium II were to be finally tested. A few days later on 4 March forty-five 'well-fleshed' male corpses specially selected from a batch gassed in Bunker II were transported to Crematorium II. The incineration rooms were on the ground floor, while in the cellar there was a gas chamber and a mortuary. Inside the incineration room the bodies were cremated under the watchful eye of Prüfer and other engineers. For the next ten days the furnaces were run to dry them out while engineers completed the gas chamber ventilation system. On Saturday, 13 March, it was announced that Crematorium II was officially operational and ready for 'special treatment'. On Sunday, 14 March, 1,492 women, children, and old people from the Kraków ghetto had been selected for the trial run at Crematorium II. Under the cover of darkness the Jews were quietly led to a temporary undressing hut built next to Crematorium II in its north yard. The trial run was a complete success and a teletype message was duly dispatched from Auschwitz informing SS headquarters that the new 'bathhouse' had undertaken its first 'special action'.

Crematorium II was only in its trial stage, and as for Crematoria III, IV and V, they were still being constructed. Nevertheless on 20 March, another transport arrived. Out of the total 3,000 Jews that arrived on that Saturday, 417 men and 192 women were selected to work, while the other 2,191 deportees were sent directly for 'special treatment'. The camp authorities had decided to use Crematorium II again for the 'special action', and in spite of some technical concerns, the selected Jews were immediately passed through the 'bathhouse'.

It immediately became apparent that the building could not handle the amount of cremations and there was an electrical fire. The ventilation system for extracting the Zyklon B from the gas chamber too developed a problem, but the SS emphatically insisted that the crematorium could not be closed down for repair. They made it known that another transport of Jews had left Salonika bound for Auschwitz and the 'special treatment' had to be carried out without delaying the schedule. On 22 March, in a drastic attempt to reduce further damage to Crematorium II, the camp authorities insisted that the architects sign off Crematorium IV while engineers tried to repair the crippled Crematorium II. When the new Salonika transport arrived, the usual selections were undertaken and those deemed unfit for work were sent straight for 'special treatment'. Nearly 2,000 Jews were led to their deaths in Crematorium IV. The killing had been so swift that the camp authorities had not even had time to trial run the incinerators.

By the end of the month Crematorium II had been temporarily repaired and transferred over to the camp again. For the next few weeks the crematoria functioned relatively well. Crematorium IV was also run simultaneously during the 'Salonika action', but because it was worked so intensively the double four-muffle furnace cracked. Eager to keep the crematoria running, engineers were immediately contacted to repair the incinerator. To make matters worse, days later the internal lining of the chimney and the connecting flue to the incinerator of Crematorium II began to collapse. While engineers tried to rectify the problem with Crematorium II, on 4 April, Crematorium V was officially handed over to camp administration. But the installation was still not deemed fully operational, since the gas-tight doors to the gas chambers were still to be fitted. Work on the doors was completed between 16 and 17 April by a civilian firm working for Huta.

With Crematoria II and IV now functioning, in mid-April SS-Sturmbannführer Alfred Franke-Gricksch, adjutant to SS-Obergruppenführer Maximillian Von Herff, Head of the SS Central Personnel Office in Berlin, who was accompanying Herff on an inspection tour of the General Government, visited Auschwitz. During his visit, Franke-Gricksch was driven to Birkenau where he toured the camp and witnessed the gassing of 2,930 Salonika Jews in Crematorium II. The procedure had gone very smoothly, but Commandant Höss was still perturbed by the crematorium breakdowns. However, in spite of the setbacks and constant bickering between the architects and engineers, in just two months both installations had in fact liquidated some 30,000 victims from the 'Salonika action', and 7,000 German, Polish and Yugoslavian Jews. Though these figures were seen as impressive to the SS any hopes to increase the capacity were quickly dashed when both crematoria were shut down in May. Crematorium II was temporarily taken out of commission so that engineers could reline the chimney, while Crematorium IV's incinerator was decommissioned.

The problems caused by crematoria's decommissioning caused incineration capacity to drop considerably. In order to cope with the amount of incoming transports destined for 'special treatment', Commandant Höss was grudgingly required to increase the open-air burnings once more. Only Crematorium I in the main camp and Crematorium V could provide limited support to the cremations.

Throughout June 1943 there were still continuous technical problems with the existing crematoria, but by 24 June Crematorium III was transferred to the camp authorities, and was back in service. Within a week Crematorium II had been brought back into operation too. By the end of June Auschwitz-Birkenau had an official daily incineration output of some 4,756 corpses. Yet, despite frequent requests by the engineers not to overload the crematoria, the Auschwitz authorities continued to operate the installations at their absolute limit. According to engineers' reports, the furnaces were not being operated correctly, being constantly overheated, and it was suggested that the Sonderkommando were deliberately damaging the internal lining with their fire irons.

During July and August recurring problems with the crematoria still continued to hamper operations. With all four crematoria running simultaneously Auschwitz had a massive killing potential, and yet only two were in operation. Crematorium IV was out of service and Crematorium II had temporarily stopped working to be repaired. Crematorium I was closed down altogether at the request of the Political Department, and as for Crematoria III and V, these two installations were running, but not at full capacity. Höss attempted everything possible to try and speed up the process of killing, fearing the camp would become quickly overcrowded with those destined for 'special treatment'. In fact, reports had confirmed that between April and the end of September 1943, Crematoria II, III, IV and V only worked for two months at full capacity. Only a quarter of their maximum capacity was used. Nonetheless, in the midst of all these problems an enormous number of people were still sent to their deaths in all four crematoria during this time. In total it is estimated that between 160,000 and 210,000 victims were given 'special treatment'.

Over the coming months, the transports into Birkenau became much larger, and the people selected for work as well as death increased massively. By May 1944, the Hungarian government reluctantly began handing over Hungarian Jews to the SS, and their destination was Auschwitz. To assist in the smooth arrival of the Hungarian Jews and to provide a direct link between the Auschwitz station and the crematoria, the railway lines were extended through the main entrance of Birkenau with plans to run them right up to Crematoria II and III. Night and day, hundreds of prisoners had been busy laying the three-way railway track through the camp, and constructing the loading and unloading ramps. By the second week of May the railway line was completed and the finishing touches were made to the ramps. From these ramps Höss would now coordinate the destruction of the Hungarian Jews, now code-named *Aktion Höss*.

The first major Hungarian transports steamed their way through to Auschwitz on 15 May. The transports varied daily, but from the very beginning of the *Aktion* until midnight on 28 May, it had been reported that some 184,049 Jews had arrived in Auschwitz in 58 trains. Within a period of just two weeks approximately 122,700 persons deemed unsuitable for forced labour were subsequently sent to their deaths. Birkenau was effectively gassing over 8,000 Jews on average each day. For the Auschwitz authorities the numbers were no less impressive for it was the most sustained mass killing so far in the history of the camp, and only comparable to the scale of murders undertaken at Treblinka during July and August 1942.

In order to ensure that the camp would not descend into chaotic disorder, Höss increased the numbers of Sonderkommando that were working in shifts in the four crematoria. By the end of May there were nearly 900 of these people living and working in the crematoria. The whole of this horrific operation was supervised only by a handful of SS men.

Throughout June more trains continued to arrive from Hungary. Though the operation was a success, the high numbers gassed began to exceed the official incineration capacity, and the crematoria were beginning to overflow with the dead. Many victims were already being burned in the pits nearby to cope with the high numbers of corpses, but Moll, who oversaw the liquidation of the Hungarian Jews, assured his superiors that the 'Moll Plan' would be achieved swiftly and successfully.

Over the coming weeks, the orgy of destruction escalated. Thousands of Hungarian Jews continued their one-way passage to the crematoria, including those who might have been valuable as labourers. Höss had observed how families had often fought to stay together during the selections, and watched with fascination how children clung to their mothers, screaming and crying. Instead of wrenching children from their mother's arms he had learnt that the best way to prevent emotional disturbances was, reluctantly, to send young and healthy women suitable for hard labour to the gas chambers with their offspring. Many Hungarian women and children went to their deaths in this way.

No matter how gruesome the outcome for these hapless Hungarian Jews during the summer of 1944, the Germans had created the perfect industrial killing factory. All four crematoria were now working more or less on a daily basis, killing thousands each day. The ovens continued to work at full capacity and the incineration ditches were being filled day and night. The frenetic gassings and burnings carried on for days and weeks regardless of the deteriorating military situation. During July an average of 3,500 each day were arriving at the ramps with more than three-quarters of the new arrivals being sent directly to the crematoria for 'special treatment'. This phenomenal figure certainly demonstrated Höss's fanatical efficiency in overseeing *Aktion Höss*. In no less than eight weeks he had masterminded the killing of more than 320,000 Hungarian Jews.

By the end of July with the number of transports dwindling the Hungarian operation ended. Orders from Budapest confirmed that the deportations were to be suspended. Just before Höss left Auschwitz on 29 July and returned to Berlin, Baer was given command of the garrison. Höss knew that Auschwitz had finally evolved, and it was now left in the capable hands of the new commander to start making plans to liquidate Birkenau section by section. One particular section that had been dis-cussed before Höss's departure was the gypsy camp. At its peak there were estimated to be some 23,000 gypsy men and women in the camp. However, thanks to overcrowding combined with the lack of food and water, disease had spread throughout the camp killing 20,000 of the 23,000 gypsies. Those remaining were rounded up on the night of 2 August and marched off to the crematoria and gassed. Höss was not present at the liquidation but he was informed by SS-Untersturmführer

Johann Schwarhuber, who was Lagerführer of the men's camp at Birkenau, that it had not been an easy task gassing them, for many had suddenly realised their fate.

In spite of the fact that by the end of 1944 the war was a lost cause for the Germans, some 500,000 prisoners were still working in German factories. Many of them were from the vast pool of prisoners in the concentration camps. At Auschwitz and the surrounding sub-camps those fit enough to be evacuated were ordered to be force-marched back to Germany and used as slave labour.

Just two months earlier the Reichsführer had ordered camps to cease extermination operations across the Reich. At Birkenau the Sonderkommando were ordered to dismantle all the killing apparatus. The incineration ditches were cleared and levelled, and pits which had been filled with ash and crushed bones of murdered prisoners were emptied and covered with fresh turf and other plantation. Crematorium I in the main camp was turned into an air raid shelter and the chimney and holes in the ceiling through which the Zyklon B was thrown in were removed. All the furnaces of Crematoria I, II, III and IV were dismantled and usable parts transported to other camps. On the night of 17 January some 58,000 prisoners were evacuated from Monowitz and the Auschwitz sub-camps, with about 20,000 coming from the Auschwitz-Birkenau. Very few were evacuated by train, with the majority being forced into the snow and marched in freezing night time temperatures westward towards Germany. As they shuffled along the icy road, behind them the night sky lit with flashes and the distant sounds of Russian gun fire rumbled across the horizon. Anyone, including children, unable to keep pace with the mass exodus was shot and their murdered corpses left at the roadside.

Amidst the chaotic evacuation, the small groups of SS left behind at Auschwitz were given instructions for the demolition of the crematoria including Bunkers I and II. After having blown up the remaining shells of Crematorium II and III in the early afternoon of 20 January, six days later they dynamited Crematorium V. As for Crematorium IV, this building had been demolished after it had been damaged by fire following a revolt in October 1944 by Sonderkommando. During the demolition of the crematoria special SS units murdered around 700 prisoners at Birkenau and nearby sub-camps. As news came of the Red Army's advance along the main road from Kraków, the guards were ordered to destroy the last of the camp records, set fire to the Canada stores and kill the remaining prisoners. However, more concerned with saving their own lives than following orders, the SS guards fled the camp leaving the soldiers of the First Ukrainian Front to liberate Auschwitz and its sub-camps. For the perpetrators, the capture of Auschwitz now reinforced their darkest fears of the retribution if caught by the Russians.

As for the Auschwitz-Birkenau site, its remains were left virtually intact, as a grim reminder of the horrors that were inflicted on the innocent souls that entered these camps.

A photograph showing the construction of the main brick entrance of Birkenau. Prisoners have been set to work to assist in its rapid build. (*Auschwitz-Birkenau Museum*)

Two photographs showing the main guardhouse to the Birkenau site. The guardhouse was attached to the main entrance to the camp.

(HITM archive & Auschwitz-Birkenau Museum)

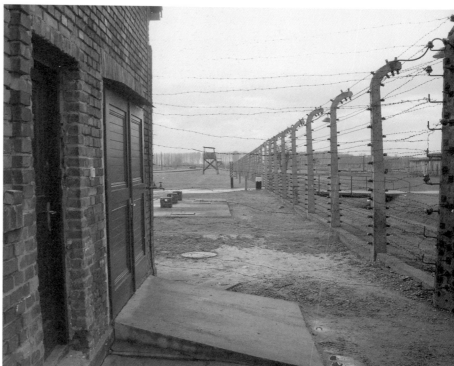

One of Auschwitz-Birkenau's prefabricated wooden guard towers along the perimeter fence of the camp.
(*HITM archive & Auschwitz-Birkenau Museum*)

(*Above*) A photograph taken from outside the main perimeter of Auschwitz-Birkenau in 2007 showing the outer camp fence and the wooden stable barracks in the designated area known as B II. (*HITM archive & Auschwitz-Birkenau Museum*)

(*Opposite and the following page*) Three photographs showing the main entrance to the Birkenau site. Construction works on the main entrance to Birkenau commenced possibly during the late winter or early spring of 1943. Originally the gate was asymmetrical, with the tower and the railway entrance as the building's northern edge. By the end of 1943, the building was further expanded to the north to create space for a transformer station. In May 1944 the commandant of Auschwitz Rudolf Höss would supervise the laying of a railway line through the main entrance for what was known as *Aktion Höss*. (*HITM archive & Auschwitz-Birkenau Museum*)

Two photographs taken in February 2007 showing the rail line through the main entrance of the Birkenau complex. The railway line was completed in May 1944 with the sole purpose of transporting Hungarian Jews directly into Birkenau. This operation at Birkenau was known as *Aktion Höss*. From the beginning of *Aktion* until midnight on 28 May it had been reported that some 184,049 Jews had arrived in Auschwitz in fifty-eight trains. *(HITM archive & Auschwitz-Birkenau Museum)*

Photograph taken in May 1944 showing Jews from Subcarpathian Rus who have been selected for forced labour at Auschwitz-Birkenau and marched to another section of the camp. (*USHMM, courtesy of Yad Vashem*)

Showing part of the rail line near the lower end of the site near Crematoria II and III. Across the complex beyond the barbed wire fence and trees that were grown to purposely conceal the lower end of the rail line and crematoria, was the area designated as the womens' camp. (*HITM archive & Auschwitz-Birkenau Museum*)

Jewish women and children from Subcarpathian Rus, who have been selected for death at Auschwitz-Birkenau, walk toward the gas chamber.
(*USHMM, courtesy of Yad Vashem*)

A photograph showing the entrance from the bottom end of the rail line of the camp leading to Crematorium II. Note the ruins of the crematorium building. (*HITM archive & Auschwitz-Birkenau Museum*)

A photograph showing the entrance from the bottom end of the rail line of the camp leading to Crematorium III. Note the ruins of the crematorium building. (*HITM archive & Auschwitz-Birkenau Museum*)

The rail line and the entrance to the complex including the guard house. (*HITM archive & Auschwitz-Birkenau Museum*)

Two photographs showing Jews from Subcarpathian Rus awaiting selection on the ramp at Auschwitz-Birkenau.
(*USHMM, courtesy of Yad Vashem*)

This photograph shows both the rail lines in the camp. At the end where the trees can be seen is where Crematorium II on the left and Crematorium III ruins stand as a grim reminder of what horrors were endured here. (*HITM archive & Auschwitz-Birkenau Museum*)

A photograph showing the rail lines and the guard house building. To the left beyond the 13ft barbed wire fence was the camp for the gypsies and Hungarian Jews. Further along was the area designated as the Theresienstadt Jews' camp. (*HITM archive & Auschwitz-Birkenau Museum*)

A transport of Jews from Subcarpathian Rus are taken off the trains and assembled on the ramp at Auschwitz-Birkenau. (*USHMM, courtesy of Yad Vashem*)

Jews from Subcarpathian Rus await selection on the ramp at Auschwitz-Birkenau. On the left is a group of uniformed prisoners from the Kanada Kommando and a few SS men. (*USHMM, courtesy of Yad Vashem*)

An entrance to the women's camp which was situated to right beyond the wooden guard house building. The area on the left was designated as B1. (*HITM archive & Auschwitz-Birkenau Museum*)

Jewish women and children, who have been selected for death, walk in a line towards the gas chambers. (*USHMM, courtesy of Yad Vashem*)

Jews from Subcarpathian Rus undergo selection at Auschwitz-Birkenau; in the background is a group of Jews headed towards the gas chambers and crematoria. (*USHMM, courtesy of Yad Vashem*)

Jewish women from Subcarpathian Rus, who have been selected for forced labour at Auschwitz-Birkenau, march toward their barracks after disinfection and head shaving. (*USHMM, courtesy of Yad Vashem*)

Three photographs showing Jews from Subcarpathian Rus undergoing a selection on the ramp at Auschwitz-Birkenau. (*USHMM, courtesy of Yad Vashem*)

Jews from Subcarpathian Rus await selection on the ramp at Auschwitz-Birkenau. In the foreground prisoners from the Kanada Kommando stand near a group of SS men. (*USHMM, courtesy of Yad Vashem*)

Jewish women from Subcarpathian Rus, who have been selected for forced labour at Auschwitz-Birkenau, wait to be taken to another section of the camp. (*USHMM, courtesy of Yad Vashem*)

A photograph showing the main SS sentry observation post. Looking across to the right is a large area designated as B IIa, b, c, d, e and f, which contained the quarantine camp, family camp for Theresienstadt Jews, camp for Hungarian Jews, men's camp, gypsy camp, and prisoner hospital area. (*HITM archive & Auschwitz-Birkenau Museum*)

Showing the same area of land during operations at Birkenau. Prisoners can be seen digging sewerage trenches in subdivision B III of Birkenau. (*USHMM, courtesy of Instytut Pamieci Narodowej*)

(*Above*) The wooden stable block houses during its operation at Birkenau. (*Auschwitz-Birkenau Museum*)

(*Opposite page*) Two photographs showing Jewish men from Subcarpathian Rus who have been selected for forced labour at Auschwitz-Birkenau. The first photo shows men awaiting further processing after having been disinfected and issued underclothing. (*USHMM, courtesy of Yad Vashem*)

(*Opposite page*) Two photographs taken during different seasons of the year, one in autumn and the other in the winter. From the main SS sentry observation post looking across to the left is the women's camp, designated as B Ia. (*HITM archive & Auschwitz-Birkenau Museum*)

(*Above*) View of the Birkenau B Ia section of the camp during its operation, from the main watch tower (Death Gate) with the Lagerstrasse on the foreground and in the background the Kartoffelbunker, the Wascheraum, Blocks 25, 26 and 27, the infirmary, remains of Block 29 for infected inmates and the x-ray block. (*USHMM, courtesy of Instytut Pamieci Narodowej*)

(*Opposite page*) Two photographs taken during two periods of the season, one in autumn and the other in the winter, from the main SS sentry observation post looking down the railway line to where Crematorium II (left) and Crematorium III (right) once stood. Right of the photograph is the area designated as B II, while to the left is the area known once as B I. (*HITM archive & Auschwitz-Birkenau Museum*)

(*Above*) SS guards walk along the arrival ramp at Auschwitz-Birkenau during its operation in May 1944. The Birkenau arrival ramp was completed only weeks before this photo was taken. Formerly the deportation trains arrived at a ramp that was 0.5 miles away. Crematoria II and III can be seen in the far background. (*USHMM, courtesy of Yad Vashem*)

(*Above*) Jews from Subcarpathian Rus undergo a selection on the ramp at Auschwitz-Birkenau. Pictured in front holding a riding crop may be either SS Unterscharführer Wilhelm Emmerich or SS Haupsturmführer Georg Hoecker assisted by a Jewish prisoner. (*USHMM, courtesy of Yad Vashem*)

(*Opposite above*) Another photograph showing the rail line from the bottom of the camp looking up to the main entrance to the complex. (*HITM archive & Auschwitz-Birkenau Museum*)

(*Opposite below*) May 1944 and Jews from Subcarpathian Rus await selection on the ramp at Auschwitz-Birkenau. (*USHMM, courtesy of Yad Vashem*)

A photograph taken in January 2006, from the main SS sentry observation post looking across to the right at large area designated as B IIa, b, c, d, e and f, which contained the quarantine camp, family camp for Theresienstadt Jews, camp for Hungarian Jews, Men's camp, Gypsy camp, and prisoner hospital area. (*HITM archive & Auschwitz-Birkenau Museum*)

The first of two photographs of the camp's former water treatment facilities. This structure was situated between Crematorium III and the Canada storage facility at the far end of the camp. (*HITM archive & Auschwitz-Birkenau Museum*)

Another photograph showing the camp's former water treatment facilities. (*HITM archive & Auschwitz-Birkenau Museum*)

A photograph taken at the far end of the camp looking across at the area designated as B II. Further beyond the barbed wire perimeter fence was an area known as B III Mexico, which was an additional part of the camp being constructed, but never completed. (*HITM archive & Auschwitz-Birkenau Museum*)

(*Above*) A photograph showing the building known as the Central Sauna, which was completed by the autumn of 1943. It entered service in December 1943 and functioned as a disinfestation facility until January 1945. The building was situated at the far end of the camp behind the storage barracks of Canada. At the Sauna, they entered the undressing room where they were medically examined and had their heads shaved. Their clothes were then sent to the autoclaves or hot air chambers. Those prisoners who had been selected for work detail were ordered to the sauna upon their arrival to the camp. They were then told to undress and shower in groups of fifty. They received a towel to dry themselves and waited for their disinfected and disinfested clothes, which they put on in the dressing room. After a final inspection by the SS they emerged from the sauna and were escorted to their designated barracks. (*HITM archive & Auschwitz-Birkenau Museum*)

(*Opposite above*) A photograph showing the Central Sauna in the distance. Note the drainage ditch. The Birkenau site was situated on marshy land, with the ground only slightly higher than the Vistula and Sola rivers. This meant that rain, melting snow and floodwaters would neither drain into the river nor be absorbed back into the earth. As a consequence hundreds of prisoners were set to work digging vast drainage ditches across the camp. (*HITM archive & Auschwitz-Birkenau Museum*)

(*Opposite below*) Lower corner of the camp showing the perimeter fence and two prefabricated wooden guard towers. (*HITM archive & Auschwitz-Birkenau Museum*)

Looking across the camp through one of the perimeter barbed wire fences are some of the many stable barracks. Many of the barracks were built from wood. A German company had designed the standard army horse stable barrack, and this was produced and dispatched to Auschwitz as a kit, where it was easily erected and dismantled. The company that had designed them said they could be assembled very rapidly with a gang of just thirty unskilled men led by one carpenter. In total 253 of these huts were assigned for Birkenau. (*HITM archive & Auschwitz-Birkenau Museum*)

Three photographs showing the area of the complex designated as B III Mexico. This area was to be the extension to the Birkenau complex. Little of this site was built, and today part of the perimeter fence still stands complete with drainage ditches. (*HITM archive & Auschwitz-Birkenau Museum*)

Drainage digging by prisoners during the operation of Birkenau. (*Auschwitz-Birkenau Museum*)

Here an iron gate leads into the camp area designated as the men's quarantine camp on the left, and on the right the family camp for Theresienstadt Jews. (*HITM archive & Auschwitz-Birkenau Museum*)

Corner of the perimeter fence of the camp complex. Looking across the camp the stable barracks were designated as part of the men's quarantine camp. (*HITM archive & Auschwitz-Birkenau Museum*)

(*Opposite page and above*) Three photographs showing the area between B II and B III Mexico. A roadway was erected that travelled the length of the camp down towards the Canada stores and beyond to the rear of the site. (*HITM archive & Auschwitz-Birkenau Museum*)

Inside the perimeter fence on the left is the area designated as the men's quarantine camp and on the right, separated by a barbed wire fence, is the family camp for Theresienstadt Jews. (*HITM archive & Auschwitz-Birkenau Museum*)

(*Above*) Jews from Subcarpathian Rus, who have been selected for forced labour at Auschwitz-Birkenau, are marched to another section of the camp. Behind them are huge piles of confiscated personal property. (*USHMM, courtesy of Yad Vashem*)

(*Opposite page*) Two photographs showing the iron gates leading into the family camp for Theresienstadt Jews. (*HITM archive & Auschwitz-Birkenau Museum*)

(*Below*) Another photograph showing the area designated as the family camp for Theresienstadt Jews. (*HITM archive & Auschwitz-Birkenau Museum*)

A photograph showing the main entrance into B II. On the left was the area known as the Hungarian Women's Camp, and on the right the men's camp. (*HITM archive & Auschwitz-Birkenau Museum*)

Looking across B II showing part of the men's camp and the gypsy camp beyond. (*HITM archive & Auschwitz-Birkenau Museum*)

Main entrance into the men's camp. (*HITM archive & Auschwitz-Birkenau Museum*)

A photograph taken through the barbed wire fence showing what is left of the men's camp. (*HITM archive & Auschwitz-Birkenau Museum*)

(*Above*) Looking along the perimeter fence of B II. In the distance is a red brick building, which was the SS administration building. (*HITM archive & Auschwitz-Birkenau Museum*)

(*Opposite above*) Looking along the perimeter fence showing what remains of the gypsy camp. Note that the drainage ditches are still in perfect working order today. In distance to the left of the birch trees is the Central Sauna building. (*HITM archive & Auschwitz-Birkenau Museum*)

(*Opposite below*) Prisoners can be seen drainage digging. (*Auschwitz-Birkenau Museum*)

(*Above*) Photographed inside the men's camp looking down towards the top end of the complex. In the distance you can see what was once the SS administration building. (*HITM archive & Auschwitz-Birkenau Museum*)

(*Opposite above*) Main entrance into what was designated as the gypsy camp. It was here in the summer of 1944 that, at its peak, an estimated 23,000 gypsy men and women were housed in this small area of the camp. However, due to severe overcrowding, combined with the lack of food and water, disease quickly spread throughout the camp killing 20,000 of them. Those remaining, including many children, were rounded up on the night of 2 August 1944, marched off to the crematoria and gassed. (*HITM archive & Auschwitz-Birkenau Museum*)

(*Opposite below*) Main roadway that separated B II and B III Mexico. To the left was the men's camp, and at the end of the road you can see what once was the SS administration building. (*HITM archive & Auschwitz-Birkenau Museum*)

(*Above*) A photograph showing the main gates at the bottom end of the complex. This road led to Crematoria IV and V and beyond that the Canada stores. (*HITM archive & Auschwitz-Birkenau Museum*)

(*Opposite above*) A good view of the drainage system that was dug by the prisoners of the camp under harsh and terrible conditions. (*HITM archive & Auschwitz-Birkenau Museum*)

(*Opposite below*) Looking across the complex at the bottom end of the camp. Hidden behind the birch trees to the right was Crematoria IV and V. In the distance is the sewage treatment works. (*HITM archive & Auschwitz-Birkenau Museum*)

(*Above*) A photograph showing what was once the SS administration building. Built in 1944, it is now converted into a Catholic Church and a school. The building is situated 0.25 miles north of the main gatehouse to the Birkenau site. (*HITM archive & Auschwitz-Birkenau Museum*)

(*Opposite above*) Remains of part of the SS administration buildings.

(*Opposite below*) Looking down towards the bottom end of the complex in the snow. To the left stands B I and to the right B II. The rail line, unloading ramp and roadway to Crematoria II and III is concealed by the snow. (*HITM archive & Auschwitz-Birkenau Museum*)

A photograph showing the perimeter fence of B I. Beyond the fence are the typical red brick barrack buildings of the what was known as the Women's Camp. (*HITM archive & Auschwitz-Birkenau Museum*)

In snow showing the prisoner stable barracks of what was known as the Men's Quarantine Camp. In the distance is the guard house entrance building to the camp. (*HITM archive & Auschwitz-Birkenau Museum*)

A photograph of the remains of what was part of the Theresienstadt Jews' camp. The brick built chimneys and the foundations are the only grim reminders of what was once here. The SS destroyed much of this area when they evacuated the camp in January 1945. *(HITM archive & Auschwitz-Birkenau Museum)*

A photograph showing the prisoner stable barracks of the Men's Quarantine Camp. Beyond are the remains of what was the Theresienstadt Jews' camp. *(HITM archive & Auschwitz-Birkenau Museum)*

(*Right*) A photograph showing the wooden lookout towers that were periodically placed across the camp complex. Armed guards with flood lights were tasked with ensuring that no prisoner attempted to escape from the camp, with a 'shoot to kill' policy. (*HITM archive & Auschwitz-Birkenau Museum*)

(*Opposite above*) A photograph showing the latrines inside one of wooden stable prisoner barracks in the Men's Quarantine Camp. Conditions for the prisoners inside these barracks were horrendous and mortality rate was considerably higher due to sickness and disease. (*HITM archive & Auschwitz-Birkenau Museum*)

(*Opposite below*) An internal view of the prisoner barracks at the Birkenau complex. All the inmates were housed in 174 barracks, each barrack subdivided into 62 bays, and each bay having a three bunk-bed system. The barracks were overcrowded and living conditions were terrible. The cold killed thousands, but even in warmer weather the mortality rate among the prisoners was high due to the lack of hygiene. The latrine system often overflowed, the sewer system did not work properly, and there were very few sick bays. (*HITM archive & Auschwitz-Birkenau Museum*)

125

(*Above*) A photograph looking across what was once the women's camp showing the red brick prisoner barracks. Note the fully-working drainage system. (*HITM archive & Auschwitz-Birkenau Museum*)

(*Opposite above*) A second photograph looking across what was left of the women's camp. Much of the red brick prisoner barracks were destroyed in 1945 leaving just the brick chimneys standing as a grim reminder. (*HITM archive & Auschwitz-Birkenau Museum*)

(*Opposite below*) A photograph showing one of the red brick prisoner barracks in the women's camp. (*HITM archive & Auschwitz-Birkenau Museum*)

Three photographs showing the brick chimney system where one of the prisoner barracks once stood. The SS did not have time to dismantle Auschwitz completely due to the rapidity of the Russian advance through southern Poland in January 1945. A number of structures were destroyed, but many of the bricks were re-used to build houses in and around the town of Birkenau and Auschwitz after the war. (*HITM archive & Auschwitz-Birkenau Museum*)

(*Above*) A photograph taken looking from the women's camp across to the main rail line down to Crematoria II and III. In the distance are the remains of the gypsy camp. (*HITM archive & Auschwitz-Birkenau Museum*)

(*Opposite above*) A photograph showing a section of the women's camp. Many of the red brick barrack buildings remain intact, both internally and externally. Each barrack was designed to house a total of 200 inmates in two sections. Each of these sections comprised of a day room, a dormitory, a washroom and a latrine area. (*HITM archive & Auschwitz-Birkenau Museum*)

(*Opposite below*) Jewish women from Subcarpathian Rus, who have been selected for forced labour at Auschwitz-Birkenau, march toward their barracks carrying bed rolls after disinfection and head shaving. (*USHMM*)

(*Above*) Taken from inside the women's camp looking across beyond the perimeter fence to the rail line. (*HITM archive & Auschwitz-Birkenau Museum*)

(*Opposite above*) A photograph showing the Birkenau sewage works. This was built to cope with the vast amount of sewage from the camp complex. It was constructed to reduce the amount of disease and sickness that plagued the camp. Round red brick basins and ditches were constructed for water purification. There were two separate sewage works or, as the Germans called it, the purification plant. These were constructed at the far end of the camp, one between the Canada store area and Crematoria II & III and the other on the other side in the corner of the camp near to Crematorium II. Inmates who complained about the stench at Birkenau often blamed the crematoria, while in reality the terrible smell came from the purification plants. (*HITM archive & Auschwitz-Birkenau Museum*)

(*Opposite below*) A photograph showing the women's kitchen building. (*HITM archive & Auschwitz-Birkenau Museum*)

(*Above*) Looking along a tract of land that divides the women's and gypsy camps. This was once a stone path area leading to a building and beyond a guard tower. (*HITM archive & Auschwitz-Birkenau Museum*)

(*Opposite above*) Looking down from the roadway near the women's camp towards the main entrance out to the unloading ramp near the rail line. If a person were to go through the iron gate and turn left, the roadway would lead to Crematoria II and III. (*HITM archive & Auschwitz-Birkenau Museum*)

(*Opposite below*) Photographed from the main iron gate entrance leading into the women's camp. A stone path travelled through the length of the camp to the perimeter fence at the top of the complex. (*HITM archive & Auschwitz-Birkenau Museum*)

(*Above*) A photograph of B1 taken from the entrance to the women's and gypsy camp areas to the opposite iron gate leading into the other section of the women's camp. (*HITM archive & Auschwitz-Birkenau Museum*)

(*Opposite above*) A photograph looking out across the women's camp towards the top end of the camp where you can see the main entrance to the camp in the distance. The red brick chimneys and the flues are all that remain after the SS blew them up during the evacuation of the camp in January 1945. (*HITM archive & Auschwitz-Birkenau Museum*)

(*Opposite below*) Looking across from inside the women's camp towards the perimeter fence. Beyond the fence is the rail line. (*HITM archive & Auschwitz-Birkenau Museum*)

(*Above*) The women's camp in B1. All of the buildings in this part of the camp were barracks constructed of red brick, stone and concrete. In late 1941, in little over five weeks, some 86,000 cubic feet of brickwork had been erected, using some 1.1 million bricks. Initially, much of the construction was undertaken using brick as there was no wood available. (*HITM archive & Auschwitz-Birkenau Museum*)

(*Opposite above*) B1 at the top end of the camp showing wooden buildings known as the Medical Barracks that were used by SS doctors and nurses including the notorious Josef Mengele. As camp physician, Mengele had a never-ending supply of human specimens on whom to experiment. Wearing his white doctor's coat and gloves, he was usually present at the selection ramps in order to single out those unfit for work. Mengele was obsessed with genetics and the theory of a Nazi master race, and he availed of the selections to hand-pick victims for participation in his sadistic medical trials. (*HITM archive & Auschwitz-Birkenau Museum*)

(*Opposite below*) A photograph taken at the top end of the women's camp. To the left is the perimeter fence of the complex where the main road runs outside the camp. (*HITM archive & Auschwitz-Birkenau Museum*)

(*Opposite above*) Looking through the women's camp towards the bottom end of the complex. (*HITM archive & Auschwitz-Birkenau Museum*)

(*Opposite below*) Photographed looking along the perimeter fence of the camp towards the main entrance to Birkenau. (*HITM archive & Auschwitz-Birkenau Museum*)

(*Above*) Looking across through the perimeter fence up towards the far end of the complex where the women's camp was situated. (*HITM archive & Auschwitz-Birkenau Museum*)

(*Above*) Looking across from near the main entrance out towards the stable barracks of the quarantine camp. To the right is the main camp perimeter fence. (*HITM archive & Auschwitz-Birkenau Museum*)

(*Opposite page*) A photograph taken from the quarantine camp looking cross towards the women's camp and medical treatment huts. (*HITM archive & Auschwitz-Birkenau Museum*)

Birch trees leading to Crematoria IV and V. In the summer of 1944 the many people who had been selected for death created long queues and were compelled patiently to sit or stand around waiting to be called through to the crematorium. Note the stone path that led through to the crematorium. (*HITM archive & Auschwitz-Birkenau Museum*)

Three photographs taken in the same area as in the previous image. These was taken in May 1944. Jews from Subcarpathian Rus wait in a clearing near a grove of birch trees before being led to the gas chambers. (*USHMM, courtesy of Yad Vashem*)

(*Above*) From the entrance of the birch trees looking across towards the bottom corner end of the camp are the remains of Crematoria IV and V. The civilian firm called Huta from Kattowitz built the shell of the crematoria. A total of about eighty men worked on the site, sixty or so were prisoners, of which twenty worked for the Auschwitz contractor Koehler on building the chimneys. In total between 100 and 150 persons, of whom the majority were prisoners, were employed on the individual work sites. While this crematorium was being built firms like Karl Falck from Gleiwitz and the Triton Company from Kattowitz handled the drainage work of the crematoria. The Klug Company from Gleiwitz helped Topf and Sons build the furnaces of Crematorium V. The SS dismantled the crematoria in late December 1944 or January 1945 and destroyed as many traces as possible of the killing operation. (*HITM archive & Auschwitz-Birkenau Museum*)

(*Opposite above*) Crematorium V in 1943. Work on Crematorium V started on 15 November 1943, and it was officially handed over on 4 April 1943. (*Auschwitz-Birkenau Museum*)

(*Opposite below*) The remains of Crematorium IV. (*HITM archive & Auschwitz-Birkenau Museum*)

(*Above*) Another photograph showing the remains of Crematorium IV. (*HITM archive & Auschwitz-Birkenau Museum*)

(*Opposite above*) A photograph taken just beyond Crematorium IV looking across an open stretch of land to the far corner of the camp. This area is where open fire pits were dug to dispose of the dead. This was undertaken when the crematoria either developed a problem, or the gas chambers were killing more than the crematoria could cope with. The main methods of lighting these huge open fire pits were petrol, methanol, crude oil and alcohol. However the special units that had been tasked with corpse disposal had in fact invented an ingenious solution. The pits had been dug with indentations at one end from which human fat could be drained off. The stokers could then pour large pails of boiling human fat over the corpses to ensure an economic and fast method of corpse disposal. (*HITM archive & Auschwitz-Birkenau Museum*)

(*Opposite below*) The construction of Crematorium IV taken by SS-man Kamann in late 1942. The architects signed off Crematorium IV on 22 March 1943.

(*Above*) Crematorium IV taken probably in September or October 1942. The main outer shell of the building is clearly being constructed along with one of the chimneys. (*Auschwitz-Birkenau Museum*)

(*Opposite above*) A photograph showing the remains of Crematorium IV. After being constructed, Crematorium IV was officially handed over to the camp administration in early April 1943, but the installation was still not fully operational, since the gas-tight doors to the gas chambers were still to be fitted. Work on the doors was completed between 16 and 17 April by a civilian firm working for Huta, and later that month became operational for murder. (*HITM archive & Auschwitz-Birkenau Museum*)

(*Opposite above*) A photograph of Crematorium IV. Work on this building started on 23 September 1942. Some nine civilian companies participated in its construction. (*Auschwitz-Birkenau Museum*)

(*Opposite page and left*) Three photographs taken from the area of Crematoria IV and V looking across to where the Central Sauna is with its perimeter fence and entrance gate. (*HITM archive & Auschwitz-Birkenau Museum*)

(*Below*) Looking from the main exit area on a road leading from Crematoria IV and V across to where the Central Sauna can be seen on the right. In the distance is the sewage treatment works. (*HITM archive & Auschwitz-Birkenau Museum*)

(*Above*) A photograph showing the still ash-blackened pools. (*HITM archive & Auschwitz-Birkenau Museum*)

(*Opposite page*) Two photographs showing the remains of what was known as the Little White House, or technically known by the SS as Bunker II. This building was the second killing facility at Birkenau. The first building, known as the Little Red House, was situated in the far north western corner of the camp where an abandoned small brick cottage with a tiled roof was found. The SS decided that the cottage, known as Bunker I, should be converted as quickly as possible. As part of the conversion, its windows and doors were to be bricked up, edges sealed with felt in order to ensure it was air-tight, and the interior gutted and formed into two rooms. The doors to both rooms were to have a sign attached over the entrance, '*Zur Desinfektion*' ('To Disinfection'). By early June 1942, in order to establish another building to exterminate prisoners, SS-Sturmbannführer Karl Bischoff and other members of the Auschwitz Construction Office discussed plans to convert a second cottage known as the 'Little White House', into what the SS called a 'bathing facility for special actions'. By the end of June this quiet and unobtrusive looking house, known as Bunker II, went into operation. The interior of the cottage comprised four narrow rooms that were constructed as gas chambers. It had improved ventilation and a killing capacity of around 1,200 people at any one time. Thousands were sent to their deaths here. (*HITM archive & Auschwitz-Birkenau Museum*)

(*Above*) Looking away from the remains of the Little White House are the foundations of the undressing station, where the victims had to undress before being led to their deaths in Bunker II. (*HITM archive & Auschwitz-Birkenau Museum*)

(*Opposite page*) A photograph showing the concrete stairs down which thousands of Jews descended prior to undressing ready to be gassed in Crematorium III. (*HITM archive & Auschwitz-Birkenau Museum*)

(*Above*) Another view of the stairs leading down to the undressing chamber of Crematorium III. The undressing chamber measured 25ft in width and 169ft in length. A roof once covered the undressing chamber. (*HITM archive & Auschwitz-Birkenau Museum*)

(*Opposite page*) Two photographs showing the ruins of Crematorium III. This building, as with all four of the crematoria built at the far end of the camp, was designed by Walter Dejaco. On the ground floor of this building were five large ovens for burning the bodies, which were brought up on an elevator. The gas chamber was not constructed underneath the cremation room but set back and reinforced by a concrete roof covered with a layer of earth so that Zyklon-B could be poured into the room through holes in the roof. (*HITM archive & Auschwitz-Birkenau Museum*)

(*Above*) Inside the undressing chamber of Crematorium III. The rubble is all that is left of the chamber's roof. (*HITM archive & Auschwitz-Birkenau Museum*)

(*Opposite page*) Two photographs showing what is left of the perimeter area where Crematoria IV and V were situated. The rail line can be seen terminating at the far end of the camp. (*HITM archive & Auschwitz-Birkenau Museum*)

(*Opposite page*) Two photographs taken in sequence showing the main path that many hapless people took once they alighted from the rail ramp. First the SS divided those that were fit for work detail and those that would be led directly to the crematoria to be gassed. (*HITM archive & Auschwitz-Birkenau Museum*)

(*Above*) A photograph showing the remains of Crematorium II. By mid-1943 this building was fully functional and murdering thousands of people. (*HITM archive & Auschwitz-Birkenau Museum*)

(*Opposite page and above*) Three more photographs showing the remains of Crematorium II.

Undressing room of Crematorium II. At the far end you can see the stairs leading down to the undressing chamber. Once undressed the Jews were directed to the other end of the dressing room into the gas chamber. This room was once covered by a flat reinforced concrete roof with earth laid on top. (*HITM archive & Auschwitz-Birkenau Museum*)

Main iron gates leading into Crematoria II and III. (*HITM archive & Auschwitz-Birkenau Museum*)

Crematorium III probably in the Spring of 1944. (*Auschwitz-Birkenau Museum*)

Jewish women and children walk toward the gas chambers. The building in the background is crematorium III. *(USHMM, courtesy of Yad Vashem)*

Photo of the sedimentation basin of BA I in the summer of 1943. Crematoria II with its blackened chimney can clearly be seen. During the height of its operation, it is calculated that some 1,140 souls per day were murdered and burned in this building. *(Auschwitz-Birkenau Museum)*

(*Above*) Prisoners pour concrete for the ceiling of the underground undressing hall of Crematoria II in the winter of 1943. (*Auschwitz-Birkenau Museum*)

(*Opposite above*) Main iron gates leading into Crematoria IV and V. (*HITM archive & Auschwitz-Birkenau Museum*)

(*Opposite below*) In memory of the thousands of innocent people that were murdered in Birkenau, flowers are laid on one of the iron gates that lead into the compound of Crematoria IV and V. (*HITM archive & Auschwitz-Birkenau Museum*)

Notes

Notes

Notes

Notes

Notes

Notes

Notes